THE FOOD AND COOKING OF
SICHUAN
AND WEST CHINA

THE FOOD AND COOKING OF
SICHUAN
AND WEST CHINA

75 regional recipes from Sichuan, Hunan, Hubei, Yunnan, Guizhou and Shaanxi, in over 370 photographs

Terry Tan

aqua marine

This edition is published by Aquamarine, an imprint of Anness Publishing Ltd, Blaby Road, Wigston, Leicestershire LE18 4SE

Email: info@anness.com

Web: www.aquamarinebooks.com; www.annesspublishing.com

If you like the images in this book and would like to investigate using them for publishing, promotions or advertising, please visit our website www.practicalpictures.com for more information.

Publisher: Joanna Lorenz
Senior Editor: Lucy Doncaster
Project Editor: Kate Eddison
Text Editors: Jenni Fleetwood and Catherine Best
Photography: Martin Brigdale
Food Stylists: Katie Giovanni and Lucy McKelvie
Prop Stylist: Martin Brigdale
Designer: Simon Daley
Illustrator: Rob Highton
Production Controller: Christine Ni

© Anness Publishing Ltd 2011

Publisher's Note

Although the advice and information in this book are believed to be accurate and true at the time of going to press, neither the authors nor the publisher can accept any legal responsibility or liability for any errors or omissions that may have been made nor for any inaccuracies nor for any loss, harm or injury that comes about from following instructions or advice in this book.

A CIP catalogue record for this book is available from the British Library.

Front cover recipe shows Crispy Chilli Beef, for recipe see page 102.

Ethical Trading Policy

At Anness Publishing we believe that business should be conducted in an ethical and ecologically sustainable way, with respect for the environment and a proper regard to the replacement of the natural resources we employ.

As a publisher, we use a lot of wood pulp to make high-quality paper for printing, and that wood commonly comes from spruce trees. We are therefore currently growing more than 750,000 trees in three Scottish forest plantations: Berrymoss (130 hectares/320 acres), West Touxhill (125 hectares/305 acres) and Deveron Forest (75 hectares/185 acres). The forests we manage contain more than 3.5 times the number of trees employed each year in making paper for the books we manufacture.

Because of this ongoing ecological investment programme, you, as our customer, can have the pleasure and reassurance of knowing that a tree is being cultivated on your behalf to naturally replace the materials used to make the book you are holding.

Our forestry programme is run in accordance with the UK Woodland Assurance Scheme (UKWAS) and will be certified by the internationally recognized Forest Stewardship Council (FSC). The FSC is a non-government organization dedicated to promoting responsible management of the world's forests.

Certification ensures forests are managed in an environmentally sustainable and socially responsible way. For further information about this scheme, go to: www.annesspublishing.com/trees

Notes

Bracketed terms are intended for American readers.

For all recipes, quantities are given in both metric and imperial measures and, where appropriate, in standard cups and spoons. Follow one set of measures, but not a mixture, because they are not interchangeable.

Standard spoon and cup measures are level. 1 tsp = 5ml, 1 tbsp = 15ml, 1 cup = 250ml/8fl oz.

Australian standard tablespoons are 20ml. Australian readers should use 3 tsp in place of 1 tbsp for measuring small quantities of gelatine, flour, salt, etc.

American pints are 16fl oz/2 cups. American readers should use 20fl oz/2.5 cups in place of 1 pint when measuring liquids.

Electric oven temperatures in this book are for conventional ovens. When using a fan oven, the temperature will probably need to be reduced by about 10–20°C/20–40°F. Since ovens vary, check with your manufacturer's instruction book for guidance.

The nutritional analysis given for each recipe is calculated per portion (i.e. serving or item), unless otherwise stated. If the recipe gives a range, such as Serves 4–6, then the nutritional analysis will be for the smaller portion size, i.e. 6 servings.

Measurements for sodium do not include salt added to taste.

Medium (US large) eggs are used unless otherwise stated in the text.

The very young, the elderly, pregnant women and those in ill-health or with a compromised immune system should not consume dishes containing raw eggs, meat or fish.

Contents

Geography and climate

The mysterious landscapes of western China are sublime and bewitching. This vast area is a humid and fertile land of cloudy mistiness, defined by expansive green rainforests, epic meandering rivers and majestic lakes, surrounded by verdant plains and foreboding mountain ranges to the west and south. The region embraces the large province of Sichuan, famous for its sizzling cuisine, as well as the municipality of Chongqing and the smaller provinces of Shaanxi, Hunan, Hubei, Guizhou and Yunnan.

West China is a landlocked area, hundreds of miles from the sea, where agriculture has been practised for centuries in a traditional style that sometimes seems untouched by the modern day. It has a large population of livestock, with pigs and chickens being the most common animals, as well as plenty of cattle, water buffalo, horses, mules and donkeys. In rural areas, sheep, goats and camels are still raised in the traditional way by nomadic herders, moving around the country to find the best grazing for their beasts.

The province of Sichuan also contains the Wolong Nature Reserve, home to the endangered giant panda. The panda's diet is exclusively bamboo leaves, while the shoots are a main part of the human population's food.

The influence of the Yangtze River

West China's heartland is the fertile Red Basin of Sichuan, surrounded by fields and mountains. Here the rainfall is predictably heavy and the climate humid, with a dampness that cloaks the air for most of the year. During the summer months, ocean-going vessels make their way up the Yangtze River as far inland as

Left Western China relies on agriculture for much of its industry, as well as fishing from the Yangtze river.
Below The western provinces of China are totally landlocked, bordering Vietnam, Laos and Myanmar, as well as the Tibet Autonomous Region.

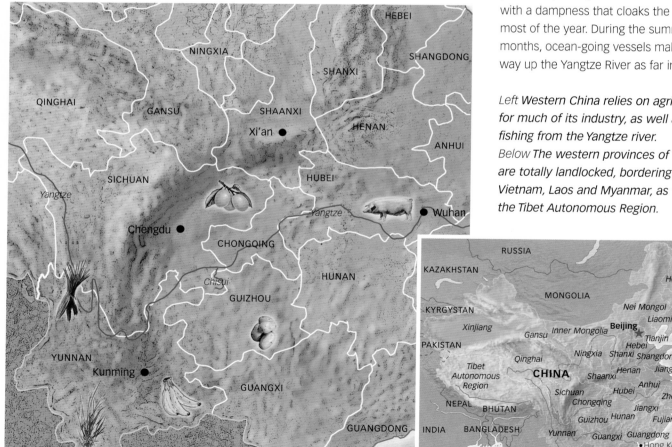

Wuhan, and flat-bottomed barges can be taken upstream as far as Chongqing, bringing with them the produce from other provinces to augment the kitchens of the area. The climate is relatively mild, with fertile soil, making the Red Basin one of the most productive, intensely cultivated and densely populated regions in China.

Most of China's rice is grown south of the Huai River, in the Yangtze valley, the Zhu Jiang delta, and in Yunnan, Guizhou, and Sichuan provinces. Rice fields, arranged in spectacular terraces, some of which date back centuries, dominate the verdant landscape. Other crops include potatoes, sweet potatoes, citrus fruits, as well as other fruits and vegetables, sugar cane, sugar beets, and green, black and jasmine teas.

Hubei and Hunan provinces are also dominated by the Yangtze River, and these fertile farmlands have been cultivated since at least the 11th century. The region was an important grain producer during the Ming and Qing dynasties. Today, Hubei is one of the largest pig-rearing provinces in China. Hunan is the birthplace of Mao Zedong, and boasts not only an exquisite cuisine but also the geographical splendour of China's second largest lake, Dongting Hu, and the soaring mountain scenery of Wulingyuan in the north-west.

On the fringes of China

Yunnan, in the far south-west of the area, has an incredible diversity of landscapes and climates. The province is framed by the Tibetan highlands at its north-western edge, and there is a mix of tropical rainforests and volcanic plains to the south, with the centre criss-crossed by hills and valleys. It is home to a third of China's ethnic minorities and, in culinary terms, has much in common with neighbouring Myanmar, Laos and Vietnam. The Dai people occupy the lush lands of the Xishuangbanna region and have been cultivating rice, sugar cane and bananas here for centuries. Their diet features esoteric ingredients such as ants' eggs and wild moss, and rice is often steamed inside hollowed bamboo stalks.

In the heart of China

Shaanxi province (not to be confused with its neighbour, the northern province of Shanxi) lies on the Loess Plateau, and is rich in natural resources, particularly coal and oil. The south of this province is a comparatively lush, mountainous area with a mild climate, whereas the north is a harsh landscape of ravines and near-vertical cliff faces where the soft soil has been eroded over the years. The Great Wall of China starts its march to Beijing in the far northern corner of this province.

Above left The Yangtze river forms the lifeline of China, winding its way through the western provinces, creating a fertile basin in Sichuan.
Above Rice terraces famously dominate the hilly landscape of Yuanyang in Yunnan province.

Guizhou province, sandwiched between Yunnan and Hunan, is a mountainous landscape of weathered limestone pinnacles that hide many of China's largest natural caverns. Despite the poor soil and over-abundant rainfall, the indigenous ethnic tribes of Miao and Dong people have managed to retain their unique lifestyle, customs and cuisine. The red-silted Chisui River – the name means 'Red Water' – runs through waterfalls and thick bamboo groves. Bamboo symbolizes the Confucian values of devotion and righteousness, and is extolled in poems and paintings for its promise of enlightenment. Local people harvest the mature stems of bamboo to make all sorts of mats and cooking utensils, and use the young shoots for cooking. Bamboo shoots in every guise – boiled, pickled, fried and steamed – pop up in every other dish. The region is also famous for its fiery alcoholic beverage, Maotai, which adds its kick to many delicious recipes.

History

The six provinces and one municipality that make up western China are some of the first areas known to be settled in historical China. This culinary history of this land dates back to at least the 5th century BC, since when the land has been inhabited and farmed. It is a fertile part of the country, making it ideal for agriculture, with abundant rain and warm weather. People initially gathered in the most hospitable valleys of the area, and some of these early village settlements became the flourishing imperial cities of later dynasties.

The name Sichuan means 'four rivers', paying reverent tribute to the important element water as dictated by feng shui (wind and water geomancy). It was established as a province in 1644 and was a base for the Chinese navy, which could use the Yangtze River to control other provinces. Today Sichuan has an enviable reputation as the foremost culinary centre of the whole area, with many dishes now famous all over the world, especially for their use of tangy, hot spices.

Early Chinese culture in Shaanxi

Shaanxi province has evidence of human civilization dating back to pre-history. It remained the political heart of China until the 9th century AD. Its capital, Xi'an, enjoyed a reputation akin to that of Rome and Constantinople as one of the greatest cities in the world. It was here that China reached the zenith of imperial power during the Tang Dynasty, established in 618. This period was truly China's Golden Age, with economic success, territorial acquisitions and political stability. Today the city of Xi'an is chiefly known for the machinations of China's infamous Qing Qin Shi Huangdi, the Yellow Emperor. He was especially noted for commissioning gigantic building projects, most notably an early version of the current Great Wall of China and the city-sized mausoleum guarded by his terracotta soldiers.

The breakaway province of Yunnan

Yunnan was the seat of the pastoral Dian Kingdom, founded in the 3rd century AD, but the province remained isolated from the rest of China for centuries afterward, resisting Han influences and maintaining its local traditions. Even today, the province is home to a third of China's ethnic minorities. The capital city of Kunming is blessed with clement weather and in ancient times was dubbed the City of Eternal Spring. It was already a thriving cosmopolitan centre by the 13th century. Within the different tribal communities are rich and unique food cultures, reflecting the distinctive characteristics of each ethnic group. The Zhuang in Yunnan form the largest group among

*Far left **The magnificent terracotta warriors of Xi'an have become famous throughout the world.***
*Left **Big Goose Pagoda in Shaanxi is an example of the fine architecture of the Qing and Ming Dynasties.***

Above Murals depicting Mao Zedong still survive on buildings in Sichuan.

China's ethnic minorities, and are particularly skilful at preparing festive dishes using ingredients such as hare, rabbit, frogs and other wild meats.

Farming in Hunan and Hubei

During the political upheavals in northern China between the 8th and 11th centuries, the fertile fields of Hunan had begun to lure millions of people to the province in search of a more peaceful life, farming and developing the land. Hunan is famous for being the birthplace of Mao Zedong, as well as for its cuisine, which is as fiery as that of Sichuan.

As early as 770BC, the province of Hubei was home to the powerful state of Chu, a culturally unique tributary state of the Zhou Dynasty. It claimed much of the middle and lower Yangtze River area, which was a rich agricultural region with an abundance of small farms on the land. Because of the landlocked topography of the region, its borders have remained relatively constant for the past 500 years. The construction of the Three Gorges Dam over the Yangtze River in 1993 brought the Hubei province into world prominence, with some controversy over the treatment of people who were displaced by the dam, as well as the environmental impact of this massive project.

Guizhou in the Qing Dynasty

The province of Guizhou was well known by the people of China for thousands of years, but did not come into world prominence until the 17th century, under the rule of the Qing Dynasty. The lush climate supports the growing of many tropical crops, including rice, maize, tobacco, tea and rapeseed. Much of Guizhou cuisine reflects the diverse but ancient culinary traditions of its 18 different ethnic minority tribes, although some of their tastes, such as the consumption of dog meat, are frowned upon today by people from other areas of China, as well as by the rest of the world.

West China in the present day

Following the Communist Party of China's victory in the Chinese Civil War (1927–50), control of the farmlands of western China was handed to the 300 million peasant farmers. In 1952 the government began organizing the peasants into mutual aid teams. In the following years, the government formally took control of the land, further structuring the agricultural areas into large government-operated collective farms. Emphasis shifted on to industrialization rather than agriculture, and today, as China continues to industrialize, huge expanses of agricultural land are being converted for industrial use, and factory work is becoming the source of income for many farmers. Despite this, western China is still one of the world's biggest food producers, and its ingredients are exported around the globe.

Below Tea plantations run along the Yangtze river in Hubei province.

Cuisine

The western area of China is known as the 'land of plenty': its agricultural fecundity is a result of the warm climate and abundant rain and river water. The great reputation of western Chinese regional cooking stems back 2,200 years, but became known to the outside world only in the second half of the 20th century. Now, Sichuan cuisine is renowned all over the globe for its depth of flavour, which centres around eye-wateringly spicy chillies, as well as piquant aromatics, sour pickles and perfectly cooked meat.

The humid climate of western China means the preservation of food takes top priority. Food may be easy to grow here, but it also deteriorates quickly unless it is preserved using a variety of techniques, from the ancient to the modern. Salting, drying, pickling, spicing and smoking all help to keep foodstuffs edible in the extreme moist heat. Aromatics such as onions, garlic and ginger feature prominently in the cuisine, as do sesame seeds, peanuts, soy bean products and fermented black soy beans. Mixed together, they produce the characteristic piquant spiciness of the region's cuisine. Throughout the whole area, the cooking embraces a diverse medley of flavours, including hot, sweet, sour and salty, and often all at once.

Spicy Sichuan cooking

Sichuan, as well as being the most populous province in western China, leads the way in the region's cooking. The cuisine of this province is often described as being a baptism of gustatory fire, and Sichuan cooking is typified by bold combinations of flavours in a single dish. Many Sichuan recipes certainly do live up to their fiery reputation, using large quantities of spicy chillies and other robust flavourings, but there are also dishes that are not touched by chillies or pungent Sichuan peppercorns. The sophistication and diversity of Sichuan cuisine is reflected in the vast range of traditional recipes, which local gourmets claim stretch to some 5000 different dishes, with

Below left Corn and chilli peppers hang in bunches outside a house in Sichuan. Below Noodles are hung up to dry in Kaili in Guizhou.

superlative examples of taste and texture. Sichuan cooks are proud of their delicious dumplings, pickled vegetables, and meat and poultry dishes that are quite unlike any other regional equivalent. Up there among the Sichuan culinary stars are dishes that were originally from the neighbouring provinces of Shaanxi, Hubei, Hunan, Guizhou and the southernmost province of Yunnan, with its intriguing mix of Han Chinese and ethnic minority tribes.

The flavoursome cuisine of Sichuan seems to successfully break all the culinary rules, mixing a whole host of pungent aromatics and intense spices. It is, however, not without logic: the careful balance of spices is not meant to burn the mouth, but to tempt the tastebuds, and to preserve foods in the hot and humid climate.

Delicacies of Hunan and Hubei
The two provinces of Hunan and Hubei share nearby Sichuan's liberal use of chillies in their cuisines. Although the cooking styles here are regarded as separate schools from that of Sichuan, they do share similar traits, especially when it comes to fiery flavours. The dishes are not always hot, but they are always complex in terms of ingredients. Hubei food has one unusual feature: the skilful blending of seafood flavours with meat and poultry, as in the unique dish Dragon Phoenix Eels with Chicken. Chefs from Hunan are masters of many ancient culinary techniques, which cover all aspects of food preparation. These include cutting meat and poultry in specific ways to suit each dish. Recipes are judged not just by taste but by aesthetics of colour, texture and visual appeal.

The pickles of Guizhou
Guizhou cuisine actually uses more chilli peppers than Sichuan, which many would find surprising. However, it is best known for the liberal use of vinegar to preserve vegetables, such as the famous Pickled Mustard Greens. There is a local folk saying: 'Without eating a sour dish for three days, people will stagger with weak legs.' Each family in Guizhou makes its own sour pickles, and these form a major part of the diet. Although it is landlocked, the province also offers some seafood dishes, including Clay-pot Fish Stew.

Above left **Vendors sell an array of vegetables at a street market.**
Above **Rice is cut and threshed on a farm in Guizhou.**

Meat and noodle dishes of Shaanxi
Shaanxi cuisine makes elaborate use of ordinary materials, particularly the staple meats, pork and mutton. Noodles take on extraordinary shapes, with some as wide as lasagne. The chief characteristics of Shaanxi cuisine are similar to those of Sichuan, but the flavours tend to be heavier and spicier. The mixture of chillies and vinegar is typical, as in all the hot-and-sour dishes of the area.

Foreign influences in Yunnan
Yunnan borders Myanmar, Laos and Vietnam and is relatively isolated from the rest of China, so the cuisine reflects many influences from the surrounding countries. This province is home to the Miao, Bai, Sami, Yi and Dai hill tribes, all of whom have their own typical methods and ingredients for favourite dishes. Rice, sugar cane, pineapples and bananas are cultivated in Yunnan province and figure prominently in the cooking.

Festivals and celebrations

Western China is a landlocked area far from the bustling, cosmopolitan centres of Beijing and Shanghai. Traditions founded here many centuries ago have persisted over the years, and certain festivals with their attendant foods are celebrated today in much the same way as they always were. From sweet almond cakes for the Moon Cake Festival to glacé fruits for the Lunar New Year, many delicate and tasty little snacks are a hugely important part of the ritual of Chinese festivals.

Festival traditions are vibrantly alive in western China, and many have huge significance in the lives of its people, often for spiritual or social reasons.

Lunar New Year
Of all the festivals, Lunar New Year is the most important. Socially, it is a time of family reunions and harmony, the burial of old feuds and tying up of loose ends. The festival is celebrated in every home, not merely as the start of a new calendar year but as a symbol of life's renewal: the old year disappears and everyone has a chance to start afresh. In the last month of the old lunar year, every home is alive with hectic preparations. Many auspicious foods are eaten, such as nuts, dates, melon seeds, glacé (candied) fruits, sugared melon slices and other sweet confections. These are presented in an eight-sided tray called the 'tray of togetherness' (*henian guanhe*). Each food on the tray invokes good fortune, prosperity, luck and all of life's positive elements. Peaches are a favourite at this time, as they symbolize a long life. The Chinese icons of Fu Lu Shu (prosperity, happiness and longevity) are portrayed in china or carved wooden figurines, and the 'longevity' figure is always holding a peach.

Water Splashing Festival
In Yunnan province, in the middle of April, a special festival is celebrated by the Dai ethnic minority group, which involves some boisterous water fun. The festival has strong echoes of the similar Thai Water Festival of Songkran, as some of the ethnic minority groups in China have close cultural ties with those of Indo-China and enjoy the same ancient traditions. The festival can last for up to five days. Prayers are said in Buddhist temples, statues of the Lord Buddha are thoroughly cleaned, and people dress up as peacocks to perform traditional dances. Best of all there is a wealth of food, such as dan dan noodles, glutinous

Below left A child in traditional dress takes part in the Lunar New Year Parade. Below Lunar New Year is celebrated in Guizhou with traditional dancing.

Above A giant moon cake is distributed free to local citizens at a special Moon Cake Festival in Chengdu.

rice dumplings in bamboo leaves, red bean paste cakes and numerous chicken dishes.

Moon Cake Festival

Throughout China, people celebrate this mid-autumn festival on the 15th day of the eighth lunar month, but the Sichuanese, with their proud food traditions, try to go one better. On one occasion in 2006, a giant moon cake was baked by the citizens of Chengdu that weighed in at an enormous 400kg (882lb). It was cut up and distributed free to the local citizens. Moon cakes are heavy, round pastries stuffed with all manner of fillings, from meat to almond paste or even salted duck's eggs. In Sichuan the classic fillings are melon seed, lotus seed and almond paste. The crusts are decorated with symbols such as dragons or a phoenix.

Right Rice dumplings are prepared for the Dragon Boat Festival in Kunming in Yunnan.

Traditionally, 13 moon cakes are piled in a pyramid to symbolize the 13 months of the lunar leap year.

Dumpling (Dragon Boat) Festival

The legend tells us that Qu Yuan, a high-ranking official of the Zhou dynasty, committed suicide after being slandered by corrupt officials. He threw himself into a river, but the people of his village, learning of this, searched the river in boats trying to find him, to no avail.

They threw rice into the river so he would not go hungry in the next life, and to stop the rice being eaten by fish, they decided to wrap the food in leaves wound tightly with silk thread so they would not come loose.

This sad event evolved into the colourful festival of today. Teams of rowers compete in races, many of their boats painted with symbols such as dragons to boost their competitive spirit. As well as the racing and feasting, according to tradition, on this day, unmarried girls would stand at their windows and throw an embroidered ball out to a crowd of unmarried men below. The man who caught the ball had to marry her – at least that's how the legend goes.

As elsewhere in China, this festival is celebrated on the fifth day of the fifth lunar month. The main festival food is rice dumplings filled with an assortment of meats and sweet bean paste, which is much loved by the Sichuan people. In the run-up to the festival, families prepare a huge range of delicious snacks such as sesame seed buns, crystal dumplings and sweet potato cakes to distribute to all the children.

Kitchen equipment

Chinese cooks have traditionally used specific pans and utensils, the shape and function of which have remained almost unchanged for centuries. The natural materials of clay, metal and bamboo are still preferred to more modern inventions for preparing and serving food, and the most popular cooking methods, such as stir-frying or steaming, rely on direct heat. The few modern culinary inventions found in Chinese kitchens, such as electric rice cookers, tend to be new versions of the older tried and tested utensils.

The simplest items, particularly a round-based wok and a heavy, sharp cleaver, are ideal for all kinds of cooking and food preparation, and will be found in every Chinese kitchen. Bamboo, a revered plant in China, is used both as a woven steamer and in the form of chopsticks.

Wok

The wok dates back centuries to the time of the nomadic tribes in northern China. These people were always on the move with their animals, searching for the best grazing sites, so they needed a utensil with a rounded base that could sit on a few rocks over a fire. The wok was born and has never changed its basic shape since then. It does multiple duty in most Chinese households as a steamer, a braising pan, a frying pan and even a shallow boiler.

Electric woks are a recent innovation, but they do not lend themselves to the high temperatures needed for quick stir-frying. However, electric woks are good for slow braising and steaming. Cast iron – an alloy of iron and carbon – is still the best material for woks, although cast aluminium, being much lighter and less expensive, is increasingly popular.

The traditional wok ladle is shaped at an angle relative to the curvature of the wok for better scooping and more efficient stir-frying, as the blade has a broader area than a wooden spoon and other conventional ladles.

Cleaver

This is a unique Chinese knife made of tempered iron or steel, honed to razor sharpness, the best size being about 30cm (12in) in length and 10cm (4in) wide, with a wooden handle, although these days they are often made from a single piece of metal. The cleaver provides essential leverage for cutting through bone and large pieces of meat, and is a versatile implement – it can be used as a carver, crusher, slicer and chopper. The blunt end serves as a makeshift mallet for tenderizing meats.

Clay or sand pot

This Chinese vessel comes with a single handle and serves as an oven-to-table utensil when food is to be served piping hot or sizzling. Traditional clay pots have

Below left **The wok is the most essential tool you will need to cook Chinese food.** *Below* **A cleaver is useful for jointing meat.**

a wire frame to support the structure, as the intense heat can cause cracks. This kind of pot is never used for the whole cooking process. Dishes are cooked in a wok or other utensils and then transferred to the clay pot, which is pre-heated just enough to maintain the temperature at the table.

Steamer
These are traditionally made of woven bamboo, but they may also be made of aluminium, with multiple perforated trays to allow the steam to come through each layer. Steamers come in many sizes, small enough to contain bitesize morsels (as in dim sum) or large enough to contain several chickens. Multiple stack steamers are ideal for cooking several dishes at the same time.

Steamboat
This kind of cooking pot originated in Mongolia, in the far north of the country. It is sometimes called a fire pot or a hot pot, and is usually made of brass-coated or enamel-coated metal, with a funnel in the centre of a moat to contain stock or water. It used to be heated over charcoal, although it is common these days to see electric models with thermostatic controls.

Various foods are cut up and placed around the steamboat so that diners can cook the food themselves in the stock, using brass wire spoons.

Bamboo draining baskets
Ubiquitous in all Asian countries, these versatile utensils are used for many purposes – as sieves (strainers), for draining soaked rice or even as food covers that allow air circulation and keep out flying insects. They are, in fact, simply the Chinese version of a colander.

Chopsticks
For many centuries, the Chinese have used bamboo chopsticks as they have a slightly rough texture, which is best for picking up slippery foods such as noodles and sauces. Normal chopsticks are 22cm (9in) long, but longer ones – up to twice this length – are used for turning deep-fried foods, keeping the user at a safe distance from spitting hot oil.

Rice cookers
These are ubiquitous in Asian homes, and are no longer regarded as a novelty in the West, as many restaurants have made use of this marvellous Japanese invention. Electric models now also have

Above left Clay pots are traditional for serving hot food in Sichuan cuisine. *Above* Bamboo steamers are the perfect vessel for cooking dim sum.

clever features for keeping rice warm for up to an hour. These work on the principle of weight – when all the liquid evaporates, the inner container, which sits on a spring-loaded element, rises automatically, switching the appliance off.

Below Chopsticks are traditionally made of bamboo.

Classic ingredients

In the cuisine of western China, certain spicy flavouring ingredients stand out and appear in almost every savoury dish. Chillies, peppercorns, onions and garlic have given the traditional cuisine of Sichuan province, in particular, its reputation for boldness and fiery heat. However, there is also a milder side, which is often overlooked by the rest of the world, focusing on the beautifully fresh ingredients that are available from the local fields and rivers, and full of more subtle flavourings.

Farmers in western China work in a rainy, warm climate, which provides ideal conditions for growing staple crops such as rice. Wheat also grows well here, giving a different emphasis to the daily diet, with more bread and noodle recipes than in other parts of China. Many dishes are spiced with chillies and Sichuan peppercorns, which give a fiery flavour to basic soups or stir-fries.

Rice
A real Chinese staple, rice is grown in most parts of the country, apart from the far north, and the western region is no exception. Rice is the single most important element in almost every meal in western China and comes in a variety of forms.

Below, left to right **Short grain rice, black glutinous rice, mung bean noodles and dried wheat noodles.**

Glutinous rice Sichuan, Hubei and Hunan chefs use this delightfully sticky cooked grain to encase savoury or sweet fillings and then wrap the whole parcel in lotus or bamboo leaves, which encase all the flavours of the dish. Black glutinous rice is also available, which gives an impressive colour to dishes.

Rice flour Many desserts have their basis in rice flour, which is made into a sort of pastry to be wrapped around bean, almond and lotus seed pastes to make tasty little sweet cakes which are then steamed or boiled. Ground rice flour is also made into rice noodles or dim sum dumpling skins.

Congee Porridge or congee is the main constituent in western China's family meals. Short grain or broken rice is cooked until it resembles porridge, with a lot of milky liquid. Congee is served with a wide range of pickles, stir-fries and simple dishes.

Noodles
While rice is the fundamental staple food in southern Chinese regions where the grain grows profusely, noodles and other wheat flour products are just as common, if not more popular, as the main staple in west China.

Mung bean noodles These always come in dried skeins that reconstitute rapidly when soaked in warm water. Their delicate looks belie their resilience: mung bean noodles remain firm and crunchy no matter how long you cook them, so they are an excellent choice for many dishes.

Wheat flour noodles These are generally yellow in colour, ranging from pale to deep golden in hue. Factories all over China produce many varieties of wheat flour noodles, both dried and fresh, and of a great many shapes and sizes, to be used in stir-fries or soups. Dried noodles are a real store-cupboard essential.

  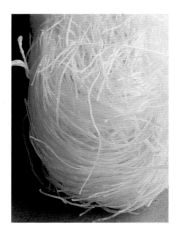 

Vegetables and herbs

Throughout China, vegetables are the most fundamental ingredient in the local cuisines, and the western provinces are no exception. Virtually every meal, no matter how grand or humble, contains some vegetables for flavour and texture as well as their nutritional value.

Beansprouts These can be eaten raw but are usually added to stir-fried noodles and cooked very briefly for their crunch, which gives a lovely contrast to the soft noodles. Their flavour is delicate and watery.

Bamboo shoots Bamboo enjoys a revered status, particularly in the western provinces of China, where it grows prolifically. The shoots are pale yellow or creamy white in colour, crunchy in texture, and have a distinctive, slightly astringent taste.

Chinese leaves These have a delicate, sweet aroma. The broad stalks are chopped for use in stir-fries, stews and soups, and sometimes they are served raw in salads.

Mooli (Daikon) This root vegetable looks very similar to a large white carrot. It is crisp, juicy and slightly spicy in flavour. It can be eaten raw or cooked and is often ground and made into a savoury cake that is served as part of a dim sum selection.

Gourds and squashes The Chinese are particularly fond of cooking with gourds and squashes, which come in a bewildering variety of shapes and sizes. They range from bitter melon with its green ridged skin to luffa squash, which has fluffy white flesh hiding within a hard green case, as well as more familiar squashes, such as courgettes (zucchini).

Above, left to right Bamboo shoots, courgettes (zucchini), mooli (daikon) and dried Chinese mushrooms.

Mushrooms These tasty fungi come in all shapes and sizes, colours and textures. Many are used fresh, while others are dried and then reconstituted, giving them a wonderfully concentrated flavour, which adds depth to many dishes. You can also buy various types of Chinese mushrooms in cans, including straw mushrooms and oyster mushrooms, which are useful store-cupboard ingredients for creating quick, tasty meals.

Mangetouts (Snow peas) These are one of the most common Chinese vegetables. They are flat, green peas, the size of a thumb; they are very crunchy and sweet and need minimal cooking. The French name, mangetout, literally means 'eat all', so these beans require no preparation.

Spring onions (Scallions) In China, these are regarded more as a vegetable than a mere garnish. They are used in quantity in many poultry dishes; they are fundamental to dumplings; and they often appear stir-fried with diced meat.

Tubers, aquatic roots and seeds Chinese cooks use tubers, roots and seeds such as cassava, ginkgo nuts, water chestnuts and lotus roots, in both sweet and savoury dishes.

Rice safety

Never keep cooked rice warm for more than a short time, or you may risk food poisoning. Rice is susceptible to a bacterium, Bacillus cereus, which is killed by cooking, but can leave behind spores that germinate if cooked rice is insufficiently reheated or kept warm for long periods of time. When buying fresh rice products, store them carefully and use within 24 hours.

Fruit

Many deciduous fruit trees such as peach, apricot, plum and chestnut have their origins in China. The western region is endowed with favourable climatic conditions and rich soils that support a plethora of temperate and sub-tropical fruits.

Apricot This tasty, soft fruit is grown widely in west China. The seeds or kernels are so sweet that they can be substituted for almonds in some recipes. The fruit is also preserved in sugar or salted as a snack.

Guava This fruit is the size of a large plum and the whole fruit is edible, from its seeds to its rind. Western Chinese people love to dip slices of guava in preserved prune powder and salt.

Lychee These delicious fruits have bumpy skins that are terracotta pink in colour. They are easily peeled to reveal juicy, gleaming white flesh, which covers a shiny, coffee-coloured seed. Sweet and fragrant, lychees are usually eaten as a simple refreshing snack on their own.

Mandarin orange These have been cultivated for centuries throughout temperate China. In western provincial cooking, the dried peel is often used as a seasoning in both savoury stews and sweet drinks.

Persimmon Also known as Sharon fruit, the persimmon is widely cultivated in sub-temperate China. They are orange in colour and the size of a mandarin. They come in two types: hard and crunchy, and soft and mushy with lots of juice.

Plum Chinese plums are sometimes eaten fresh, but most often end up pickled, dried, salted or puréed into plum sauce. Salted or glacé (candied) plums that resemble sultanas are favourite snacks throughout China.

Tofu and tofu products

Few other foods stimulate the creativity of Chinese chefs more than humble tofu and its variations. Tofu, or beancurd, is made from soaked, mashed and strained soya beans, and is white in colour. As old as Chinese culinary history itself, tofu is a highly nutritious product that lends itself to a multitude of recipes, especially as it comes in many forms.

Fresh tofu The soft variety of fresh tofu, sometimes branded as silken tofu, can be eaten just as it is, requiring no more than gentle blanching or steaming over boiling water. It is delicate and so cannot withstand harsh cooking techniques. The firm variety is best in stir-fries and as fillings, as it is much more robust and will hold its shape when cooked. Tofu takes up other flavours very well.

Above, left to right **Pineapple, firm tofu, pork belly and beef fillet.**

Dried tofu Also known as beancurd sticks in China, this creamy white vegetarian staple is made by simmering soy bean milk until a thin skin forms on top. This skin is then lifted off very carefully and hung out to dry. It features in many nourishing soups and stews from Sichuan.

Fried tofu This type of tofu is made by deep-frying firm tofu until a brown skin forms. It can form a pocket for meat or seafood stuffing, or is simply shredded and added to congee. In Sichuan and Hubei, fried tofu is a main ingredient in many vegetarian stews.

Fermented tofu To make fermented tofu, fresh tofu is left to dry out in the sun. Then salt, Chinese grain wine and spices are added to it. Fermented tofu is a favourite condiment in western China, which is traditionally served with rice congee, in a marinade for poultry or as a rich seasoning that is used in braised dishes.

Tofu skins and wafers When tofu is being made, the skin that begins to form on the surface is carefully lifted and dried to become thin, parchment-like light brown sheets. These are used as spring roll wrappers with a special texture and flavour.

Meat, poultry and eggs

Although many western provincial dishes feature lamb, beef and game, pork remains the main thread that runs through the cuisine of meat dishes in these regions.

Pork Roast pork is made from a rib cut that is streaked with the requisite amount of fat and cut as a wide, long strip, whereas the hock or leg cut is usually used for braising. Sichuan and Hunan chefs are past masters at using particular cuts, such as pork belly and ribs, which have a perfect ratio of fat and lean meat for the recipe.

Beef Stir-fries with beef often contain bamboo shoots, that quintessential Chinese vegetable, as well as fiery Sichuan chillies and peppercorns. Fillet, rump, sirloin, rib-eye and stewing steak are all used by western Chinese chefs.

Offal Western provincial cooking elevates the art of cooking offal to exceptional heights, for example in the dishes lungs with shredded bamboo shoots, liver with wine and garlic, and kidneys in soup with ginger.

Poultry The range of chicken dishes throughout western China is virtually endless, with hundreds of different recipes. If cooked whole, chicken is

Below, left to right Duck breast, pig's kidneys, prawns (shrimp) and carp.

usually braised, steamed or simmered gently in a stew with ginseng or other herbs. More often, chicken is cut into small pieces before cooking. Pigeons and quail are often steamed, deep-fried or stewed with medicinal herbs. Duck is famously used in Chinese cooking; the wonderful Aromatic Crispy Duck is one of Sichuan's most famous dishes.

Eggs Duck eggs are often eaten as century eggs, or salted and boiled, served with rice congee.

Fish and shellfish

Western provincial fish cookery is rich in taste and intriguing in method and ingredients. Salted, dried, pickled aromatic spices and vegetables are fully employed as seasonings for fish and shellfish. When combined with sesame oil and fermented soy bean sauces, they produce the characteristic piquant spiciness that is famed in western Chinese cooking.

Shellfish Although much of western China is completely landlocked, many varieties of shellfish have freshwater cousins that can be caught in the rivers and lakes. Crabs such as mud crabs or mottled crabs turn up in many seafood compotes, stir-fries and soups. Western Chinese cuisine features prawns (shrimp) in a great many dishes, such as as Jade Prawns Chengdu-style and Paper-wrapped Prawns.

Jointing a chicken

Many recipes specify a jointed chicken and, although you can buy them ready prepared, it is quite easy to joint a bird at home. You will need a large sharp knife and poultry shears for cutting through meat and bone.

1 Put the chicken breast-side up on a chopping board. Use a sharp knife to remove the leg by cutting through the skin and then through the thigh joint. Repeat with the leg on the other side.

2 Following the line of the breastbone, and using poultry shears, cut the breast in half, making the cut as clean as possible.

3 Turn the bird over and cut out the backbone. Leave the wings attached.

4 Cut each breast in half, leaving a portion of the breast attached to the wing.

5 Cut each leg through the knee joint to separate the thigh and drumstick.

6 Using poultry shears, cut off the wing tip at the first joint.

River fish In the river tributaries of west China, freshwater fish are plentiful. From the inland rivers come freshwater wrasse, mudfish, perch, trout, pike, carp and sturgeon. In Sichuan and other western provinces, whitebait or sprats can be found in the rivers. They are so small they can be eaten whole, or they can be dried and stored for the winter months.

Herbs, spices and flavourings

Chinese cuisine is full of strong and surprising tastes, often derived from a subtle combination of seasoning ingredients. The appearance of the dish is also a major consideration, and herb and spice garnishes are central to Chinese food.

Black beans Soy beans are roasted and fermented with salt, and sometimes also with ginger, until black and very pungent. They are then left whole or ground into a thick paste to be used as a condiment.

Chillies Fresh or dried, chillies are fundamental to western Chinese cooking. They come in many varieties, from the mild and bland to the really hot with their high-octane kick, and Sichuan cooking is almost synonymous with the spiciness of chillies.

Chilli bean paste This thick, spicy mixture is made of a purée of ground dried chillies blended with yellow bean paste. It is originally from Sichuan, where

Peeling and deveining raw prawns

Raw prawns (shrimp) must have their intestinal tracts removed before cooking, a process that is known as 'deveining'. It is not necessary to devein very small shrimp.
1 Pull off the head and legs from each prawn, then carefully peel off the body shell with your fingers. Leave on the tail 'fan' if you like.
2 Make a shallow incision down the centre of the curved back of the prawn using a small sharp knife, cutting all the way from the tail to the head.
3 Carefully pick out the thin black vein that runs the length of the prawn with the tip of the knife and discard.

it is known as dou banchiang. It gives a flavourful kick to many western Chinese dishes.

Dried anchovies or whitebait Tiny dried fish such as anchovies and whitebait are fundamental in Sichuan and Hunan cooking, as a rich flavouring for soups, or simply fried and made into a hot sauce with chilli paste.

Dried shrimps Small shrimps are dried until they are completely dehydrated and a dusky pink in colour. They must be soaked before cooking, and are widely used in Sichuan and Hunan cuisine for their unique taste.

Fermented beancurd This comes in two types: red and white. Both types taste extremely salty and pungent. Red fermented beancurd is essential for red-cooked dishes and as a seasoning and colorant for roast meats.

Ginger This is available in two forms: young tender stems of a pale yellow colour with green stalks, or ginger roots with a light brown thin skin. Ginger is integral to stir-fries and as a condiment in dips.

Hoisin sauce This is made from a blend of yellow bean paste and sugar, and is coloured a rich, dark mahogany. Its most common use is as a rub on pancakes with Aromatic Crispy Duck from Sichuan or the similar Peking duck, which originated in Beijing.

Sesame oil This strong-flavoured oil is widely used in western Chinese cooking, mainly as a top note in soups and stir-fries. It has an aromatic and nutty fragrance, adding depth of flavour to many dishes.

Below, left to right Whitebait, ginger, red fermented beancurd and hoisin sauce.

Sesame seeds These tiny seeds come in a variety of colours, from creamy white to charcoal black. They can be ground to a paste, imparting a subtle perfume, but are most often sprinkled on stir-fries just before serving, such as the delicious Sesame Beef from Hubei, which can also be made with pork, too.

Sichuan peppercorns These reddish-brown pungent peppercorns are indigenous to western China. They are very strong, with a slight hint of liquorice flavour. They are used in many recipes on the Sichuan menu, and make an attractive garnish when ground and sprinkled on top of the dish.

Soy sauce This has become a major part of all regional Chinese cooking and is also very popular throughout the rest of the world today. It is made of soy beans and comes in dark, light, reduced salt, thick or thin varieties. It adds essential colour and flavour to stews, casseroles and marinades, and features in the vast range of braised poultry and pork dishes typical of western China. This is one Chinese staple that you will definitely need in your store cupboard.

Vinegars Black and red vinegars are essential seasonings throughout western China. They are used widely as the basic souring agent in soups, and are served on their own as tasty dips for dumplings and fried foods.

Tea

People in western China are great tea drinkers. Yunnan, the south-western province closest to Myanmar and Vietnam, is the birthplace of tea; it has the ideal climate, with a perfect rooting medium in the red clay soil. In Hunan province, too, red and black teas are grown along the foothills of the mountains. Tea is used for steaming fish, poultry and meat, with each tea providing a distinctive flavour.

Black tea This type of tea is first fermented, or oxidized. When it is only semi-fermented, it is known as oolong tea. Black tea is generally stronger in flavour and contains more caffeine than the less oxidized teas.

Green tea This is an unfermented tea and is simply dried in the sun or in special drying kilns, where the leaves may also be steamed to make them soft. The finest green teas are still hand-processed today.

Alcoholic drinks

Archaeological digs in China have dated the existence of alcohol here as far back as 4,000 years ago. Certainly by the 11th century, wine-making from fruits and grains was an industry all over present-day China. The Chinese production of alcoholic beverages is split between grain alcohol, beer and wine.

Above, left to right Red vinegar, sesame seeds, Mei Kuei Lu and green tea.

Beer Although historical records show that both wine and beer have been made in China for thousands of years, beer drinking has only become really popular in the last 30 years. Today, probably the best-known Chinese beer is from Qingdao: it is commercially known as Tsingtao, which is its brand name, and it is now available throughout the world.

Grain wines Given their intensity of alcohol, most grain wines are, in reality, closer to spirits. Fermented grain wine may be clear or yellowish-brown in colour; white liquor is the distilled beverage made from glutinous rice. Most Chinese love rice wine, and it is used for both drinking and cooking throughout the western region. Shaoxing wine is the most common type of rice wine, and is the one used in the vast majority of recipes.

Maotai Arguably the most famous Chinese liquor, Maotai is known as the spirit of China. Its name literally means 'thatched terrace', and it originated during the Qing dynasty in a village of the same name situated in the Guizhou province of western China. The area is especially famous for its long history of winemaking.

Soups and dim sum

Wonderfully adaptable, soups and dim sum play a variety of roles throughout China, and neither are limited to being served as appetizers. Soups can be served as a taste teaser, as a refreshing interlude between mouthfuls of richer dishes or, as is common in western China, at the end of the meal to cleanse the palate after the intense Sichuan flavours. Dim sum, or dian xin, as it is known in Mandarin, is the collective name for small bites and snacks, both sweet and savoury, and is intrinsically linked with the tradition of tea drinking.

Cleansing soups and fiery bites

Soups in western China tend to be surprisingly mild, giving a refreshing and cleansing break from the hot and spicy flavours of Sichuan cuisine. One exception to this rule is the iconic Hot-and-Sour Soup, which is thick, intensely flavoured, and full of chicken and tofu chunks. Others are milder, such as Corn Soup, or they are delicately flavoured with pickled and salted vegetables. In Guizhou, cooks are particularly adept at using fish to enhance their soups.

Dim sum, which translates as 'food to touch the heart', comprises a wide range of dumplings wrapped in a variety of different pastries. As the chief characteristics of this regional school of cooking lie in the frequent and lavish use of various soy bean pastes, these are invariably used in the seasonings for dim sum, making them richer than those of other regions. Soy sauces, sesame oil, peppercorns and oyster sauce are touched with wine and other alcoholic beverages for heady measure.

Snacks such as Sweet Potato Cakes are sold on the streets in Chengdu, and Glutinous Rice Balls with Sesame Paste appear unfailingly during the Lunar New Year as a festive must. In a culinary triumph, Jicama Dumplings have, over the past century, crossed not only regional borders but also oceans: they are now a favourite in restaurants throughout South-east Asia.

Whatever type of dim sum is served there will always be the requisite dipping sauces, such as black vinegar with ginger, garlic, salt and oil (and usually some fiery chilly paste added), to accompany it.

Serves 4

200g/7oz firm-fleshed fish fillet,
  such as monkfish or cod,
  membrane or skin removed
45ml/3 tbsp groundnut (peanut) oil
4 garlic cloves, sliced
1 garlic clove, crushed
800ml/1½ pints/scant 3¼ cups
  boiling water
30ml/2 tbsp light soy sauce
2.5ml/½ tsp finely ground
  Sichuan peppercorns
small bunch of watercress or
  shredded lettuce leaves

Spicy fish soup

A Guizhou staple, this soup of monkfish or cod with crisp garlic makes a light but aromatic first course. Any type of firm-fleshed fish can be used, but monkfish is particularly good, as it has the texture of chicken and no tiny bones to worry about. The spicing comes from the famous Sichuan peppercorns, known for their liquorice flavour and subtle fire, as well as the liberal quantity of garlic.

1 Cut the fish into 5mm/¼in thick slices. Heat the oil in a large, heavy pan and fry the garlic slices until golden brown. Lift out the garlic using a slotted spoon and set aside. In the remaining oil, fry the crushed garlic for 30 seconds until golden brown.

2 Add the boiling water to the pan and then add the fish, soy sauce and Sichuan peppercorns. Return to the boil, then simmer for 2 minutes, then add the watercress or lettuce and simmer for 1 minute or until the fish is cooked. Serve garnished with the fried garlic.

Cook's tip This soup can be made with an equal quantity of shellfish, such as raw, shelled prawns (shrimp) or scallops, which makes it an attractive choice for entertaining.

Per portion Energy 138kcal/572kJ; Protein 8g; Carbohydrate 1g, of which sugars 0g; Fat 11g, of which saturates 2g; Cholesterol 7mg; Calcium 5mg; Fibre 0.2g; Sodium 9mg

Hot-and-sour soup

This Sichuan soup has crossed more borders in China than the Great Wall and it has become a part of Hunan and even Cantonese cooking. The blend of black Xinkiang (or Sinkiang) vinegar, chopped chillies and pepper is aromatic and spicy, and it really catches the throat. Generally chicken is added, but a vegetarian version can feature just the diced tofu. Long-life tofu is available in two types – silken and firm; either are suitable.

1 Pour the boiling water into a pan and cook the chicken breast for 10 minutes. Lift out using a slotted spoon and dice into small 1cm/½in cubes.

2 Return the chicken cubes to the stock and add all the remaining ingredients except the cornflour and garnish. Bring to the boil, then reduce the heat to a simmer and cook for 5 minutes. Taste and adjust the seasoning.

3 Put the cornflour in a small bowl and blend with a little cold water. Stir into the soup and cook, stirring, until thickened. Serve topped with fried onions or garlic slices.

Cook's tip Xinkiang vinegar has a distinctive sharp taste and is very different from ordinary white vinegar. If this is not available, use a good dark wine vinegar. The characteristic hue of this soup is a dark amber.

Serves 4

800ml/1½ pints/scant 3¼ cups
  boiling water
1 skinless chicken breast fillet,
  about 125g/4¼oz
50g/2oz silken or firm tofu,
  cut into 1cm/½in cubes
30ml/2 tbsp Xinkiang black vinegar
2.5ml/½ tsp ground Sichuan
  peppercorns
2 fresh red chillies, finely chopped
1 spring onion (scallion),
  finely chopped
30ml/2 tbsp light soy sauce
2.5ml/½ tsp caster (superfine) sugar
15ml/1 tbsp cornflour (cornstarch)
salt and ground black pepper
fried onions or garlic slices, to garnish

Per portion Energy 65kcal/275kJ; Protein 9g;
Carbohydrate 5g, of which sugars 2g; Fat 1g,
of which saturates 0g; Cholesterol 22mg;
Calcium 73mg; Fibre 0g; Sodium 655mg

Corn soup

This well-loved recipe is believed to have originated in Hubei, but since there have been centuries of cuisines crossing borders, it is difficult to establish this with any historical accuracy. In a further complication, you can find this soup in just about every Chinese restaurant from Sydney to San Francisco. Whatever its origins, it makes a great dish. Chicken is used here, although pork is another favourite. This recipe uses fresh corn for authenticity as well as flavour and texture – it is so much tastier than canned corn, which is generally used to make the soup in takeaways.

1 Stand each cob on end and, using a sharp knife, slice the kernels off as close to the cob as possible, then scrape as much juice out of the cob as you can and pour it into a blender. Add the kernels, cornflour and half the stock, then blend for 1–2 minutes, or until almost smooth. Set aside.

2 Put the remaining stock into a large, heavy pan and add the chicken. Cook, covered, over a low heat for 15 minutes. Lift out the chicken using a slotted spoon and cut into small dice or tear into small shreds.

3 Return the chicken to the pan and add the corn mixture. Bring to the boil, then reduce the heat and simmer, stirring frequently, for 6–8 minutes, or until slightly thickened and the cornflour has cooked. Season with sesame oil and salt to taste.

4 Using a wooden spoon, stir the simmering soup in circles with one hand while you pour in the lightly beaten eggs in a thin stream with the other. The egg will form thin threads. Serve immediately, garnished with shredded or chopped spring onion.

Serves 4

2 corn on the cob, as fresh
  as possible
15ml/1 tbsp cornflour (cornstarch)
500ml/17fl oz/generous 2 cups light
  chicken stock
1 skinless chicken breast fillet
10ml/2 tsp sesame oil
2 eggs, lightly beaten
salt and ground white pepper
1 shredded or chopped spring onion
  (scallion), to garnish

Cook's tip If you prefer your soup to be thickened without cornflour, simply leave it out – the corn's natural starches will provide some thickening.

Per portion Energy 185kcal/777kJ; Protein 14g; Carbohydrate 15g, of which sugars 2g; Fat 8g, of which saturates 2g; Cholesterol 138mg; Calcium 28mg; Fibre 1.3g; Sodium 448mg

 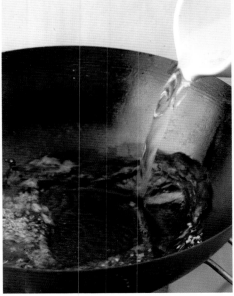 

Chicken soup with pickled greens

Pickled (or salted) mustard greens are eaten throughout most of China and are used not only as a vegetable, but as a salting agent as well. They are never served alone but always in soups or stews, or they will be stir-fried with egg and pork. In Chinese wet markets (rural predecessors to supermarkets), the greens are sold in large earthenware crocks; elsewhere, they are available vacuum-packed or canned in most Chinese stores.

1 Cut the pickled greens into thin strips, wash in plenty of cold water and squeeze them dry. If you want to reduce the salt content, leave the greens to soak in cold water for an hour or so before use.

2 Heat the oil in a large, heavy pan and fry the garlic for 30 seconds or until golden brown. Add the boiling water and chicken breast, boil for 10 minutes, then lift out the chicken using a slotted spoon and shred into thin strips.

3 Return the shredded chicken to the stock and add the sesame oil. Add the mustard greens to the soup with the rice wine or vinegar, and sugar, and simmer for 4 minutes. Taste and add soy sauce if needed. Serve hot.

Cook's tips
• The quality of canned and vacuum-packed mustard greens can vary: sometimes you will find mostly stalk and very few leaves, whereas others have plenty of soft leaves. Generally speaking, the vacuum-packed greens are the best quality.
• You may not need to add the soy sauce, as the salted mustard greens may be sufficiently salty for your taste.

Serves 4

2 or 3 pickled mustard green pieces
30ml/2 tbsp groundnut (peanut) oil
2 garlic cloves, crushed
800ml/1½ pints/scant 3¼ cups
  boiling water
1 skinless chicken breast fillet,
  about 125g/4¼oz
15ml/1 tbsp sesame oil
15ml/1 tbsp rice wine or vinegar
2.5ml/½ tsp caster (superfine) sugar
15ml/1 tbsp light soy sauce,
  or to taste

Per portion Energy 73kcal/307kJ; Protein 8g;
Carbohydrate 1g, of which sugars 1g; Fat 4g,
of which saturates 1g; Cholesterol 22mg;
Calcium 4mg; Fibre 0.1g; Sodium 286mg

Pork balls in clear soup

Minced pork has a wide range of uses in Chinese cuisine, and here it is mixed with cloud ears and flavourings, then formed into tiny pork balls to be cooked in soup. Minced pork from the supermarket is not ideal, as it will not have the correct ratio of fat to lean meat that gives the best flavour and succulence. For an authentic soup, it is best to make your own mince for the pork balls, using one-third fatty pork belly and two-thirds shoulder meat.

1 Rinse and drain the cloud ears, then snip off the tough parts with kitchen scissors and chop the remainder finely. Put into a large bowl.

2 Heat the oil in a small pan over a medium-low heat and fry the shallots, stirring frequently, until they are crisp and brown. Drain on kitchen paper and set aside.

3 Add the spring onion to the bowl with the cloud ears, then add the minced pork, cornflour, soy sauce and pepper. Mix well.

4 Shape the mixture into small balls the size of large grapes.

5 Put the stock into a large pan and bring to the boil, then turn down to a vigorous simmer over a medium-low heat. Add the pork balls and simmer for 4–5 minutes, or until cooked through and they have risen to the surface. Season the soup with salt to taste and serve hot, sprinkled with the fried shallots and some fresh coriander or chopped spring onions.

Cook's tip Normally, 200ml/7fl oz/scant 1 cup of liquid will fill a typical Chinese rice bowl. When you add the other ingredients this quantity of stock will serve nicely as a first course, giving you about 250ml/8fl oz/1 cup soup.

Serves 4

4 cloud ear (wood ear) mushrooms, soaked in lukewarm water for 10–15 minutes
45ml/3 tbsp vegetable oil
3 shallots, very thinly sliced
1 spring onion (scallion), finely chopped
200g/7oz minced (ground) pork
5ml/1 tsp cornflour (cornstarch)
5ml/1 tsp light soy sauce
2.5ml/½ tsp ground black pepper
800ml/1½ pints/scant 3¼ cups meat stock
salt
coriander (cilantro) leaves or chopped spring onion, to garnish

Per portion Energy 180kcal/745kJ; Protein 12g; Carbohydrate 4g, of which sugars 1g; Fat 14g, of which saturates 2g; Cholesterol 32mg; Calcium 12mg; Fibre 0.2g; Sodium 734mg

Sweet potato cakes

In Chengdu, many versions of these little fried cakes are popular as street food. Some are a simple blend of sweet potato and rice flour, as here, whereas others are filled with lotus seed or red bean paste. They are very easy to make and you can eat them dipped in honey or even with ice cream. Look for sweet potatoes with an orangey flesh. No sugar is needed as sweet potatoes, as their name indicates, are naturally sweet.

1 Preheat the oven to 180°C/350°F/Gas 4. Place the sweet potatoes on a baking tray and bake for 45 minutes–1 hour, or until soft. (Steaming them can make them watery.)

2 Leave the potatoes to cool slightly, then halve them and scoop as much flesh as possible into a bowl. Discard the skins. While still warm, mash the flesh until smooth, then add the glutinous rice flour and mix to make a smooth dough, adding more flour if necessary.

3 Heat the oil for deep-frying over a medium heat. Pinch off walnut-size pieces of dough and roll in cornflour to coat very lightly. Deep-fry a few balls at a time, stirring so that they fry on all sides, until they bob to the top of the oil and turn golden brown. Lift out with a slotted spoon or wire basket and drain on kitchen paper. Serve warm or cold, with honey.

Variation You can also roll the balls in sesame seeds before deep-frying, if you like. These are also delicious with ice cream and golden (light corn) syrup or maple syrup drizzled over.

Makes about 20

500g/1¼lb orange-fleshed sweet
  potatoes, unpeeled
about 115g/4oz/1 cup glutinous rice
  flour or wheat starch
vegetable oil, for deep-frying
cornflour (cornstarch), for dusting
honey, to serve

Per portion Energy 75kcal/315kJ; Protein 1g;
Carbohydrate 11g, of which sugars 1g; Fat 3g,
of which saturates 0g; Cholesterol 0mg;
Calcium 8mg; Fibre 0.7g; Sodium 11mg

Serves 4

115g/4oz plain (all-purpose) flour
1 egg
pinch of fine salt
60ml/4 tbsp vegetable oil

For the filling
175g/6oz sesame seeds
15ml/1 tbsp lard or white cooking fat
40g/1½oz caster (superfine) sugar

Per portion Energy 590kcal/2451kJ; Protein 13g;
Carbohydrate 33g, of which sugars 11g; Fat 46g,
of which saturates 7g; Cholesterol 61mg;
Calcium 343mg; Fibre 4.3g; Sodium 130mg

Sesame seed pastries

These sweet pastries with their sesame seed filling are more like pancakes, with a slightly savoury flavour to balance out the sugar. In Mandarin they are called ping, which can often refer to any small pastry.

1 To make the filling, put the sesame seeds into a dry pan and stir over a medium heat for 8–9 minutes, or until pale golden. Grind the warm toasted seeds to a paste using a food processor, grinder or mortar and pestle, then add a few drops of water to make a stiff paste.

2 Heat the lard or white cooking fat in a wok over a medium heat, add the sugar and cook until it has dissolved. Add the sesame seed mixture and cook for 2 minutes over a low heat to obtain a smooth, thick paste. Transfer the paste to a plate, and leave to cool completely.

3 Sift the flour into a large bowl and make a hollow in the centre. Beat the egg and salt together in a small bowl and add to the well in the centre of the flour. Pour in 200ml/7fl oz/ scant 1 cup water and whisk everything quickly together to make a thick but flowing batter.

4 Grease a non-stick frying pan with some of the oil and set it over a medium-low heat. Pour in 60–75ml/4–5 tbsp batter to make a thin pancake. Cook until set on top, then flip over and cook for 10 seconds. Transfer to a plate. Use the remaining batter to make more pancakes.

5 Spread 15ml/2 tbsp of the filling on to the centre of each pancake. Fold opposite sides into the centre, then the top and bottom to make a parcel. Heat the remaining oil in a large frying pan over a medium heat. Quickly fry the folded pancakes until crisp and golden on both sides. Cut into slices and serve warm or at room temperature.

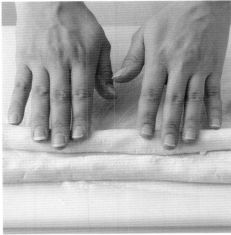

Glutinous rice balls with sesame paste

Known as tang yuan in Sichuan, Hubei and other parts of China, these light rice balls are integral to the Lunar New Year festival. In rural Sichuan and Hubei, they are still made in a time-honoured way, which involves soaking glutinous rice for several days and then grinding it in a large granite grinder. Water is then squeezed out through layers of muslin (cheesecloth) until a wet dough is left. These days, glutinous rice flour is a labour-saving option.

1 To make the filling, put the sesame seeds into a dry pan and stir over a medium heat for a few minutes until light golden. Grind the toasted sesame seeds until fine, using a mortar and pestle, then stir in the sugar.

2 Heat the lard or white cooking fat in a wok, add the sesame seeds and fry the mixture over a low heat until you get a creamy texture. Set aside, cool, then chill, covered, until needed.

3 Put the two rice flours into a large bowl and stir in 200ml/7fl oz/scant 1 cup warm water to make a soft dough. Divide the dough into three pieces and roll each on a floured board into a sausage shape about 2.5cm/1in thick.

4 Pinch off small pieces of dough the size of large grapes: the dough should make 20 balls. Flatten each piece to make an indentation in the centre.

5 Place a teaspoonful of paste in each piece of dough and draw over the sides to make small balls. Shape and smooth the balls to make them neat.

6 Bring a large pan of water to the boil and cook the dough balls for about 15 minutes, or until they float to the surface.

7 Meanwhile, boil 1 litre/1¾ pints/4 cups water in a pan and add the winter melon slices. Cook for 5 minutes. Divide this sweetened water among serving bowls. Using a slotted spoon, transfer the cooked rice balls to the serving bowls; there should be 5 per serving.

Serves 4

200g/7oz/1¾ cups glutinous
  rice flour
30ml/2 tbsp rice flour
90g/3½oz crystallized winter melon,
  sliced, to serve

For the filling
20g/¾oz/scant ⅛ cup sesame seeds
20g/¾oz/1½ tbsp caster
  (superfine) sugar
10ml/2 tsp lard or white cooking fat

Cook's tips
• At step 1, instead of toasting and grinding the sesame seeds, you can use the equivalent amount of light sesame seed tahini. Depending on the type you buy, adjust with sugar to taste and heat to blend.
• You can also add a few drops of vanilla extract to the melon water, to add a subtle fragrance, if you like.

Per portion Energy 335kcal/1402kJ; Protein 5g; Carbohydrate 65g, of which sugars 19g; Fat 6g, of which saturates 1g; Cholesterol 2mg; Calcium 51mg; Fibre 1.6g; Sodium 8mg

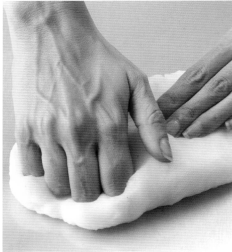

Jicama dumplings

The filling for these dumplings is made with jicama, a root vegetable that resembles a large, sweet turnip with a thin brown skin. It tastes faintly of crunchy water chestnuts and goes well with prawns and soy sauce in these light, steamed dim sum.

1 To make the filling, slice the jicama rounds into thin strips, then wash and drain well. Soak the dried prawns in warm water for 15 minutes, then crush with a mortar and pestle.

2 Heat the oil in a wok or heavy pan and fry the garlic for 30 seconds. Add the jicama, soy sauce, pepper, dried prawns and 200ml/7fl oz/scant 1 cup water. Cook over a medium heat for 20 minutes, or until almost dry – the jicama should be soft but not mushy. Drain off the excess juices if necessary. Remove from the heat and leave to cool.

3 Put the wheat starch or rice flour in a large pan (preferably non-stick) with 25g/1oz/¼ cup cornflour and gradually stir in the boiling water. Keep stirring over a low heat until the dough is smooth, then remove from the heat. Add the remaining cornflour and the oil. Add a little more water, if necessary, as you work the dough until it becomes slightly elastic and moist.

4 When cool enough to handle, transfer the dough to a floured board and knead well, punching the dough occasionally to make it very light.

5 Shape the dough into a long roll about 5cm/2in in diameter. Divide into ten pieces about 2.5cm/1in thick and flatten each with a rolling pin until about 5mm/¼in thick. Place 1 heaped tablespoonful of filling slightly off-centre on each dough circle. Fold over the dough to make a half-moon shape and moisten the edges. Pinch to seal the edges.

6 Trim off the excess dough and crimp the edges with the tines of a fork. Place on a lightly oiled plate and transfer to a steamer over simmering water. Steam for 30 minutes. Serve warm with a thick, sweet soy sauce.

Makes 10

75g/3oz wheat starch or glutinous rice flour, plus extra for dusting
90g/3½oz/generous ⅔ cup cornflour (cornstarch)
about 250ml/8fl oz/1 cup boiling water
15ml/1 tbsp vegetable oil
sweet soy sauce, to serve

For the filling
250g/9oz jicama, peeled and thinly sliced into rounds
25g/1oz/2 tbsp dried prawns (shrimp)
45ml/3 tbsp groundnut (peanut) oil
2 garlic cloves, crushed
30ml/2 tbsp light soy sauce
5ml/1 tsp ground black pepper

Per portion Energy 123kcal/513kJ; Protein 1g; Carbohydrate 16g, of which sugars 1g; Fat 6g, of which saturates 1g; Cholesterol 5mg; Calcium 19mg; Fibre 0.8g; Sodium 227mg

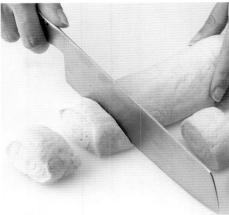

Pork and cabbage dumplings

These dumplings are Hubei staples that are eaten as snacks. Unlike Western dumplings, they are usually made with self-raising flour and dry yeast. The filling is a mild blend of fried minced pork and cabbage flavoured with pepper, garlic and soy sauce.

1 Sift the flour into a large bowl and stir in the yeast, salt and sugar. Make a well in the centre and pour in the warm water. Stir the water into the dry ingredients to form a slightly sticky dough, then knead for 10 minutes on a floured surface. Return to the bowl, cover with a damp dish towel, and leave in a warm place to rise for 30–40 minutes, or until doubled in bulk.

2 Gently turn the dough over to deflate it, then cover and leave for a further 15 minutes. Meanwhile, make the filling. Fill a pan with boiling water and plunge in the cabbage leaves for 45 seconds–1 minute, or until just limp. Drain thoroughly in a colander, then squeeze the leaves to remove the excess moisture. Finely chop the cabbage.

3 Heat the oil in a wok or pan over a high heat and fry the garlic for 30 seconds. Add the minced pork and chopped cabbage, and fry for 1 minute. Add the soy sauce, pepper, sugar, salt and 100ml/3½fl oz/scant ½ cup water, then cook for 3 minutes, or until the filling is nearly dry. Spread the filling on to a plate to cool completely.

4 Press out the dough into a rectangle on a floured surface. Roll it up tightly into a log about 5cm/2in in diameter, then cut into 12 slices. Dust a slice with flour and, with a small rolling pin, roll it out into a round 9cm/3½in in diameter, making the edges slightly thinner than the centre.

5 Place a heaped teaspoonful of filling in the centre of the round and bring up the sides to enclose the filling, ruching and gathering up the edge as you rotate the dumpling in your palm. Pinch the gathered-up top tightly to seal, and pinch off the excess dough, leaving a neat little button. Make the remaining dumplings in the same way.

6 Cut 12 5cm/2in squares of baking parchment. Place each dumpling on a parchment square, then transfer to a steamer over simmering water. Steam over a high heat for 15 minutes.

Makes 12

200g/7oz/1¾ cups self-raising (self-rising) flour, plus extra for dusting
15g/½oz/1 tsp easy bake (rapid-rise) yeast
pinch of salt
5ml/1 tsp caster (superfine) sugar
120ml/4fl oz/½ cup warm water

For the filling
75g/3oz white cabbage leaves
30ml/2 tbsp groundnut (peanut) oil
2 garlic cloves, crushed
90g/3½oz/scant ½ cup minced (ground) pork
30ml/2 tbsp dark soy sauce
2.5ml/½ tsp ground black pepper
2.5ml/½ tsp caster (superfine) sugar
1.5ml/¼ tsp salt

Variation For a richer flavour, halve the amount of soy sauce and add 15ml/1 tbsp oyster sauce.

Per portion Energy 95kcal/401kJ; Protein 4g; Carbohydrate 14g, of which sugars 1g; Fat 3g, of which saturates 1g; Cholesterol 5mg; Calcium 64mg; Fibre 0.7g; Sodium 291mg

Fish and shellfish

Western China is composed of landlocked provinces, but despite the scarcity of the saltwater fish that are the culinary hallmarks of the southern and eastern coastal regions, fish and shellfish cooking has nonetheless made a terrific impact within the spectrum of the cuisine. Fish leap from their placid rivers, lakes and muddy paddy fields, and shellfish lurk in crevices beneath the calm waters, ready to be marinated, braised, stir-fried or deep-fried. Local cooks claim that the finest flavours come from river fish, whether wild or farmed.

Spicy squid and braised fish

Western Chinese cooks are skilled at making the most of flavourful local fish. Although some farmed fish from inland lakes and paddy fields are often tainted with the scent of mud, they are nevertheless used by adept chefs: the fish are simply left to swim in tanks of clean water before they are prepared. The region's humidity affects many of the cooking styles, and the preservation of food takes top priority. Salted, dried and pickled aromatics and vegetables are fully employed as seasonings for fish and shellfish. When combined with sesame oil and fermented soy bean sauces they achieve the piquant flavours for which the area is renowned.

Shellfish come into their own in the cooking of this region: prawns (shrimp) are marinated in wine, braised, stir-fried or even wrapped in rice paper before being deep-fried; and squid and octopus are drenched in fiery chilli sauce. Regional cooks embrace a medley of flavours, including hot, sweet, sour and salty, and often all at once. The foods of Sichuan, Hunan and Hubei are well documented for their fiery promise.

Excess fish and shellfish are often processed into cakes and balls, and steamed or fried as main courses or snacks. Small fish like anchovies and whitebait are dried and stored for the lean winter months, and are used frequently as stock ingredients, due to their rich flavour. Chrysanthemum Fish Hot Pot is a rich compendium of intoxicating flavours perfumed with chrysanthemum petals and leaves, and uses several varieties of fish and shellfish.

Chrysanthemum fish hot pot

In China, autumn-flowering chrysanthemum leaves are used to perfume this glorious, richly flavoured seafood dish, which is commonly served in autumn throughout western China. The bitesize pieces of food are traditionally cooked in simmering stock at the table in a charcoal-heated fire pot (huo kuo). As burning charcoal is not suitable indoors, use an electric fire pot or steamboat instead, or a large fondue pan over a burner.

1 Soak the fish maw in hot water for about 10 minutes, until it swells. Drain and cut into bitesize pieces. Thinly slice the softened mushrooms. Put all the raw fish ingredients and the mushrooms, tofu, chrysanthemum leaves and mangetouts on to small plates or in bowls and arrange around a fire pot or steamboat on the table.

2 To make the dips, mix the black vinegar with the garlic, ginger and sesame oil. Spoon into a small bowl. Put the chilli sauce and soy sauce into small bowls and place on the table. Heat the fire pot or steamboat at the table.

3 Pour the stock into a large pan and bring to the boil, then carefully transfer to the fire pot or steamboat and season with the Sichuan pepper and the salt. Keep the stock simmering at the table.

4 Each diner takes morsels of food from the plates or bowls and either spears them on to a long fork or puts them into a brass wire spoon. The food is then submerged in the boiling stock until cooked, then eaten with the accompanying dips.

5 When all the food has been cooked, serve the rich stock in bowls as a soup.

Cook's tips
• You can use water instead of stock, if you like. This will give you a lighter stock, but it will still have a good flavour from the ingredients that have been cooked in it.
• Fish balls, fish cakes and fresh chrysanthemum leaves can be bought from Chinese stores. Chrysanthemum petals, due to their delicate nature, are rarely imported from China.

Serves 8–10

90g/3½oz fish maw (dried fish bladder)
10 dried Chinese mushrooms, soaked
 in warm water for 30 minutes
200g/7oz cod or halibut fillet,
 thinly sliced
20 Chinese fish balls
2 large Chinese fish cakes, sliced
10 raw tiger prawns
 (jumbo shrimp), shelled
350g/12oz pack silken tofu
90g/3½oz chrysanthemum leaves
 (tong ho)
90g/3½oz mangetouts (snow peas)
2 litres/3½ pints/8 cups meat stock
5ml/1 tsp ground Sichuan peppercorns
5ml/1 tsp salt

For the dips
60ml/4 tbsp Xinkiang black vinegar
15ml/1 tbsp crushed garlic
15ml/1 tbsp finely grated ginger
5ml/1 tsp sesame oil
chilli sauce
soy sauce

Per portion Energy 100kcal/422kJ; Protein 15g;
Carbohydrate 6g, of which sugars 1g; Fat 2g,
of which saturates 0g; Cholesterol 41mg;
Calcium 142mg; Fibre 0.6g; Sodium 1396mg

Clay-pot fish stew

Monkfish, mushrooms, tofu and mangetouts are cooked in a sauce strongly flavoured with garlic, hoisin and oyster sauces and served in a traditional clay pot, which is used throughout China to keep the food beautifully hot. The dish will first be cooked in a pan and then transferred to the preheated clay pot, then covered with its lid. If you don't have a clay pot, you can use a flameproof casserole heated on the top of the stove or in the oven.

1 Preheat a clay pot or flameproof casserole on the stove for a few minutes or in the oven heated to 200°C/400°F/Gas 6 for 10 minutes. Cut the fish into 2.5cm/1in chunks and slice the softened mushrooms.

2 Heat the oil in a wok over a medium heat, then add the garlic and fry for 1 minute. Add the mushrooms and fried tofu, then stir-fry for 2 minutes. Add the wine, hoisin sauce and oyster sauce and fry for 1 minute, then add 200ml/7fl oz/scant 1 cup water and bring to a simmer.

3 Add the fish and simmer gently, stirring frequently, for 2–3 minutes, or until it is just cooked. Add the mangetouts and cook for 1 minute more. Put the cornflour in a bowl and blend with 15ml/1 tbsp water, then add to the wok and cook for a few seconds until the sauce boils and thickens. Season with salt and white pepper.

4 Preheat a clay pot or flameproof casserole over a direct flame for a few minutes or in a hot oven for 10 minutes. Transfer to the clay pot and serve, garnished with fresh coriander.

Cook's tips
• Clay pots are simple cooking vessels that are not made to last a lifetime, so be careful not to overheat it or it might crack.
• You can buy fried tofu already prepared in cubes from most Chinese stores. The cubes are light brown and hollow inside.

Serves 4

350g/12oz monkfish (or similar firm-fleshed fish), membrane removed
8 dried Chinese mushrooms, soaked for 30 minutes in warm water
30ml/2 tbsp vegetable oil
3 garlic cloves, crushed
8 pieces of fried tofu (see Cook's Tip)
30ml/2 tbsp Chinese wine
15ml/1 tbsp hoisin sauce
30ml/2 tbsp oyster sauce
16 mangetouts (snow peas)
10ml/2 tsp cornflour (cornstarch)
salt and ground white pepper
fresh coriander (cilantro) sprigs, to garnish

Per portion Energy 238kcal/995kJ; Protein 20g; Carbohydrate 11g, of which sugars 2g; Fat 12g, of which saturates 1g; Cholesterol 12mg; Calcium 324mg; Fibre 0.6g; Sodium 506mg

Braised grouper in chilli sauce

Grouper is highly prized for its exquisite flesh and crisp, flavourful skin when fried, as here. It belongs to a large family of fish found widely in warm waters, especially along coral reefs, but they also thrive in temperate climes, in deep oceans and river estuaries.

1 Using a sharp knife, score deep cuts across the thickest part of the fish, then dust with cornflour and shake off the excess. If you do not have a wok large enough to hold a whole fish, cut the fish into two pieces down the middle.

2 Heat the vegetable oil in a wok or deep-fryer, then add the fish in batches if necessary and deep-fry until golden brown. Set aside.

3 To make the sauce, heat the oil in a large wok or frying pan, then add the ginger and spring onion and fry for 1 minute. Add the chilli bean paste, sugar, chillies and soy sauce, then fry for 30 seconds.

4 Add the wine and 300ml/½ pint/1¼ cups water, then bring to the boil. Lower the fried fish into the sauce to simmer for 2 minutes. The initial coating of cornflour will fuse with the sauce to thicken it.

5 Transfer the cooked fish pieces to a serving platter, arranging them to make the whole fish, and sprinkle with chopped spring onions or fresh coriander before serving.

Variation If you prefer not to deep-fry the fish it can be cooked in the sauce for 8 minutes, or until cooked through. This will give a different texture to the fish.

Cook's tip You can buy decorative Chinese vegetable cutters to make pretty mooli garnishes.

Serves 4

2 whole grouper (675g/1½lb total
  weight), cleaned and fins removed
60ml/4 tbsp cornflour (cornstarch)
vegetable oil, for deep-frying

For the sauce
30ml/2 tbsp vegetable oil
30ml/2 tbsp grated fresh root ginger
1 spring onion (scallion), chopped
45ml/3 tbsp chilli bean paste
  (dou banjiang)
5ml/1 tsp caster (superfine) sugar
2 fresh green chillies, seeded
  and sliced
15ml/1 tbsp light soy sauce
30ml/2 tbsp Chinese wine
shredded spring onion and mooli
  (daikon) decorations (see Cook's
  Tip), to garnish

Per portion Energy 430kcal/1796kJ; Protein 41g;
Carbohydrate 18g, of which sugars 4g; Fat 21g,
of which saturates 3g; Cholesterol 0mg;
Calcium 281mg; Fibre 0.2g; Sodium 688mg

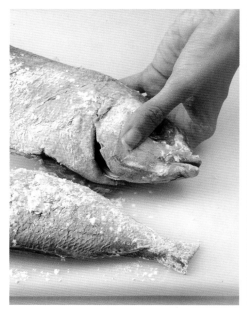  

Braised fish with garlic

Being closely affiliated with Sichuan, Hunan cooking has much in common with her sister province and is often even more fiery. The spiciest variety of chilli that grows here is a fingertip-sized pod called 'to the sky', as it grows facing upward. Shaoxing wine, Sichuan pepper, ginger and spring onions make up the classic marinade described as xian, which defies translation: it is indefinable and utterly intoxicating.

1 With a very sharp knife, make a few parallel slashes through the thickest part of the fish on both sides. Dust the snapper evenly with cornflour, shaking off the excess.

2 Heat the oil in a large wok or frying pan and shallow-fry the fish over a medium heat until well browned, turning once. (The fish will not be fully cooked on the inside.) Set aside.

3 Drain off all but 15ml/1 tbsp oil from the pan. Add the garlic, ginger and peppercorns to the oil in the pan, then increase the heat to high and fry for 1 minute.

4 Add the spring onions, wine or sherry, soy sauce, rice wine or vinegar, sugar and 400ml/14fl oz/1²/₃ cups water. Bring to the boil and cook for 2–3 minutes to reduce the liquid and intensify the flavours.

5 Return the fried fish to the pan, and reduce the heat to medium. Partially cover the pan and braise the fish for 3 minutes. Turn the fish over, add the chillies and cook for a further 2 minutes, until the sauce has reduced and thickened and the fish are cooked through.

6 Season the sauce with salt to taste and serve immediately, garnished with shredded spring onions.

Serves 4

2 whole snapper (675g/1¹/₂lb total weight), cleaned and fins removed
30ml/2 tbsp cornflour (cornstarch)
120ml/4fl oz/¹/₂ cup vegetable oil
8 garlic cloves, halved
25g/1oz fresh root ginger, thinly sliced
2.5ml/¹/₂ tsp Sichuan peppercorns
2 spring onions (scallions), cut into 5cm/2in lengths
30ml/2 tbsp Shaoxing wine or dry sherry
15ml/1 tbsp dark soy sauce
10ml/2 tsp rice wine or vinegar
5ml/1 tsp caster (superfine) sugar
salt
2 fresh red chillies, finely chopped
shredded spring onions, to garnish

Per portion Energy 257kcal/1075kJ; Protein 21g; Carbohydrate 11g, of which sugars 2g; Fat 14g, of which saturates 2g; Cholesterol 37mg; Calcium 54mg; Fibre 0.3g; Sodium 397mg

Tofu fish in a spicy sauce

Texture is fundamental to Chinese cuisine, although Westerners sometimes find this a little difficult to appreciate fully. For the Chinese, however, it is every bit as important as flavour and colour, and is often described as kou kan, which is loosely translated as 'mouth feel'. In this dish, kou kan is highlighted in the contrasting textures of soft tofu with the crispness of the fried fish combined in a hot chilli sauce.

1 Cut the fish into 2.5cm/1in cubes. Heat 60ml/4 tbsp oil in a wok over a high heat. When very hot, add the tofu cubes and fry, turning frequently, until well browned. Lift out using a slotted spoon and drain on kitchen paper.

2 Reduce the heat to medium and add the fish to the remaining oil. Fry for 4 minutes, gently turning the cubes a few times, until they are lightly browned all over and almost cooked through. Transfer to a plate and set aside.

3 Wipe the wok using kitchen paper and add the remaining oil. Add the garlic and fry for 1 minute, then add yellow bean sauce, soy sauce, chillies and sugar, and fry for 1 minute.

4 Add 150ml/¼ pint/⅔ cup water and simmer for 1 minute, then return the fish and tofu to the wok. Cover and cook for 1 minute more, until the fish is cooked through. Serve immediately, sprinkled with spring onion.

Cook's tip For an extra crunchy texture you can add a handful of mangetouts (snow peas) or 30ml/2 tbsp shredded cooked bamboo shoots when you return the fish and tofu to the wok in step 4.

Serves 4

600g/1lb 6oz monkfish or cod fillet,
  or any firm-fleshed fish,
  membrane or skin removed
75ml/5 tbsp vegetable oil
200g/7oz firm tofu, cut into
  2cm/¾in cubes
2 garlic cloves, crushed
15ml/1 tbsp yellow bean sauce
15ml/1 tbsp dark soy sauce
3 fresh red chillies, seeded and sliced
5ml/1 tsp caster (superfine) sugar
1 chopped spring onion (scallion),
  to garnish

Per portion Energy 340kcal/1418kJ; Protein 31g; Carbohydrate 6g, of which sugars 2g; Fat 22g, of which saturates 3g; Cholesterol 21mg; Calcium 280mg; Fibre 0.1g; Sodium 2189mg

Five-spice carp

Carp is a favourite freshwater fish often used in Chinese cooking, and in this Sichuan dish it is flavoured with ginger and the quintessential Chinese seasoning, five-spice powder. Although classically termed 'five-spice', the powder may contain more than just five, but the main ingredients are star anise, cinnamon or cassia bark, Sichuan pepper, fennel and cloves, which give the dish a pronounced flavour.

1 Coat the carp liberally with cornflour and shake off the excess. Heat the vegetable oil for deep-frying in a wok or deep-fryer to 190ºC/375ºF and add the carp. Deep-fry until crisp. Lift out carefully and drain on kitchen paper.

2 Heat a large frying pan or the cleaned wok with the 30ml/2 tbsp vegetable oil and fry the ginger for 1 minute. Add the sesame oil, soy sauce and sugar, and stir for 30 seconds.

3 Add the wine or sherry to the wok or pan with the rice wine or vinegar, five-spice powder and 75ml/5 tbsp water. Stir well. Put the drained fish into the sauce, spooning the sauce over liberally. Simmer for 1–2 minutes, or until well heated through.

4 Serve hot, garnished with chopped spring onions and whole coriander leaves.

Serves 4

1 large carp (about 600g/1lb 6oz),
  cleaned and fins removed
30ml/2 tbsp cornflour (cornstarch)
30ml/2 tbsp vegetable oil
25g/1oz fresh root ginger, chopped
15ml/1 tbsp sesame oil
30ml/2 tbsp dark soy sauce
2.5ml/½ tsp caster (superfine) sugar
30ml/2 tbsp Shaoxing wine or
  dry sherry
5ml/1 tsp rice wine or vinegar
2.5ml/½ tsp five-spice powder
vegetable oil, for deep-frying
chopped spring onions (scallions) and
  coriander (cilantro) leaves, to garnish

Per portion Energy 318kcal/1326kJ; Protein 21g;
Carbohydrate 9g, of which sugars 1g; Fat 22g,
of which saturates 3g; Cholesterol 75mg;
Calcium 61mg; Fibre 0 g; Sodium 483mg

Sweet-and-sour carp

Each province, town, and even family, has its own version of sweet-and-sour sauce. The universal sauce of perfectly balanced contrasting flavours is unique to the culinary heritage of China and essential to many dishes. In Chengdu restaurants, sweet-and-sour sauce with carp is the pièce de résistance, using the Sichuan sweet-and-sour combination that includes Shaoxing wine (the more subtle Cantonese version uses a blend of fruity and sour flavours from plum and vinegar). This recipe is for a whole fish but tastes just as wonderful with fillets.

1 Using a sharp knife, make deep gashes into the thickest part of the fish, then put the fish into a shallow dish. Put the marinade ingredients in a bowl and mix well together. Rub liberally over the outside and inside of the fish, then set aside for 20 minutes.

2 Lift the fish from the marinade and then coat it with the cornflour. Heat the vegetable oil for deep-frying in a wok or deep-fryer and fry the fish until the skin is golden brown and crisp. Lift out and drain on kitchen paper.

3 Fry the sliced garlic and shredded ginger until golden brown, then drain.

4 Put the sweet-and-sour sauce ingredients in a bowl and mix well, then pour into a small pan and cook over a low heat until the sugar has dissolved.

5 Transfer the sauce to a clean wok and add the fried garlic, shredded ginger and spring onions. Add the fried fish and turn once or twice so that it is well coated in the sauce. The sauce will thicken from the cornflour coating. Serve the fish with the sauce poured over.

Variation To give the sauce a fruity flavour, use 30ml/2 tbsp plum sauce instead of the caster sugar.

Serves 4

1 large carp (about 600g/1lb 6oz),
  cleaned, or same weight of fillets
75g/3oz/²⁄₃ cup cornflour (cornstarch)
3 garlic cloves, sliced
15ml/1 tbsp shredded fresh root ginger
2 spring onions (scallions), cut into
  5cm/2in lengths
vegetable oil, for deep-frying

For the marinade
30ml/2 tbsp Shaoxing wine or dry sherry
2.5ml/½ tsp salt
1 garlic clove, crushed
5ml/1 tsp finely grated ginger

For the sweet-and-sour sauce
15ml/1 tbsp light soy sauce
60ml/4 tbsp caster (superfine) sugar
15ml/1 tbsp Shaoxing wine or dry sherry
30ml/2 tbsp Xinkiang black vinegar
15ml/1 tbsp sesame oil
pinch of salt

Per portion Energy 334kcal/1402kJ; Protein 21g;
Carbohydrate 30g, of which sugars 11g; Fat 14g,
of which saturates 2g; Cholesterol 75mg;
Calcium 67mg; Fibre 0.2g; Sodium 620mg

Fish in hot sweet-and-sour sauce

Sweet-and-sour sauce is given some fire with the addition of the rich red chilli bean paste, called dou banjiang, which is characteristic of many Sichuan dishes and found in every kitchen in the region. The best dou banjiang is said to come from the town of Pixian, outside Chengdu, but most grocery stores sell a variety of brands. It's salty and hot, and a little of it goes a long way – but it's just right with crispy cod or halibut.

1 Cut the fish into slices about 1cm/½in thick, then pat them dry with kitchen paper. Dust the slices lightly with potato flour. Heat the vegetable oil in a wok over a medium heat or in a deep-fryer, then add the fish, in batches if necessary, and deep-fry until golden brown, about 2–3 minutes per batch. Lift out and drain on kitchen paper, then set aside.

2 In the same oil, deep-fry the ginger strips for several seconds, until light brown. Drain on kitchen paper and set aside.

3 To make the sauce, put the chilli bean paste in a small bowl and blend in the sugar, rice wine or vinegar, soy sauce and 250ml/8fl oz/1 cup water. Pour into a wok or frying pan and bring to a simmer over a medium heat. Add the sliced leek and cook for 1–2 minutes, or until it is tender but still crisp.

4 Add the fish and stir gently to mix well. Garnish with the fried ginger and serve immediately.

Variation Seed and slice 2 fresh red chillies and add to the sauce with the leeks for extra fire, if you like.

Serves 4

675g/1½lb cod, halibut or monkfish
  fillets, or other firm-fleshed white
  fish, skin or membrane removed
60ml/4 tbsp potato flour or any
  starchy flour
25g/1oz fresh root ginger, cut into
  fine strips
vegetable oil, for deep-frying

For the sauce
30ml/2 tbsp chilli bean paste
  (dou banjiang)
10ml/2 tsp caster (superfine) sugar
30ml/2 tbsp rice wine or vinegar
15ml/1 tbsp light soy sauce
1 leek, thinly sliced

Per portion Energy 347kcal/1450kJ; Protein 33g;
Carbohydrate 17g, of which sugars 5g; Fat 17g,
of which saturates 2g; Cholesterol 78mg;
Calcium 28mg; Fibre 1.5g; Sodium 571mg

Crispy hot whitebait

Sichuan provincial towns and villages are criss-crossed with rivers, and the people who live there can often be seen with small nets catching whatever happens to be swimming by. Freshwater fish of all kinds, usually small fish and shrimps, are then deep-fried and sold as snacks. Here, the fried fish are given a spicy seasoning using Sichuan peppercorns, chillies and ginger.

1 If the whitebait are frozen, thaw and drain them thoroughly in a sieve (strainer). Pat very dry with kitchen paper – if they are at all damp they will not crisp up when fried.

2 Put the Sichuan peppercorns for the seasoning in a dry pan and toast for 1 minute. Grind to a powder using a mortar and pestle, then transfer to a small bowl. Coarsely grind the chillies and add to the peppercorns. Add the remaining seasonings and stir until well blended. Set aside.

3 Heat the vegetable oil for deep-frying in a wok over a medium heat or in a deep-fryer. Put the flour and potato starch into a large plastic bag and shake to combine, then add the whitebait and shake well to coat the fish completely. Transfer the floured whitebait to a sieve (strainer) and shake gently to remove the excess flour.

4 Deep-fry the whitebait in batches for about 1 minute per batch, until crisp and golden brown. Drain well on kitchen paper and keep warm. Sprinkle the seasoning over the whitebait and toss well to coat. Garnish with spring onions and serve immediately.

Variation Tiny shrimps in their shells, each no more than 2cm/¾in across, are also delicious prepared this way – eat them shell and all.

Serves 4

600g/1lb 6oz whitebait
90g/3½oz plain (all-purpose) flour
15ml/1 tbsp potato starch
vegetable oil, for deep-frying
finely chopped spring onions
   (scallions), to garnish

For the seasonings
2.5ml/½ tsp Sichuan peppercorns
5ml/1 tsp coarsely ground
   dried chillies
2.5ml/½ tsp caster (superfine) sugar
5ml/1 tsp sesame oil
2.5ml/½ tsp salt
15ml/1 tbsp fresh root ginger, grated
   and ground to a paste

Per portion Energy 672kcal/2783kJ; Protein 25g;
Carbohydrate 8g, of which sugars 1g; Fat 61g,
of which saturates 0g; Cholesterol 0mg;
Calcium 1077mg; Fibre 0.3g; Sodium 534mg

Dragon phoenix eels with chicken

The dragon and phoenix are both rich with symbolism and are favourite metaphors for certain types of food. The phoenix, which represents the female, is likened to the chicken and rebirth; prawns (shrimp) and fish represent the male and are symbolic of the dragon. Essentially, however, these metaphors serve to emphasise the Chinese gift for combining seafood and poultry in one dish, as in this Hubei dish of eels and chicken. Eels are usually bought while still alive, as their flavour deteriorates rapidly once dead. They are difficult to prepare, so ask your fishmonger to do this for you.

1 Heat the oil in a wok and fry the spring onions and ginger for 1 minute. Lightly crush the fermented tofu and add to the pan. Fry for 30 seconds.

2 Add the eel and chicken strips and stir-fry for 2 minutes, then add the oyster sauce, sugar, sesame oil, wine or sherry, and mangetouts. Stir-fry for a further 2 minutes.

3 Add 200ml/7fl oz/scant 1 cup water, bring quickly to the boil and cook for 5 minutes. Add the spring onions, then stir for 20 seconds. Serve immediately, garnished with coriander.

Variation Monkfish or conger eel are good substitutes for brown eel, as they have the same meaty texture.

Serves 4

30ml/2 tbsp groundnut (peanut) oil
2 spring onions (scallions), white part
  only, chopped
20g/³⁄₄oz fresh root ginger, shredded
1 cube red fermented tofu (tofu ru)
450g/1lb brown eels, cut into
  thick strips
300g/11oz skinless chicken breast
  fillet, sliced into thick strips
30ml/2 tbsp oyster sauce
5ml/1 tsp caster (superfine) sugar
30ml/2 tbsp sesame oil
30ml/2 tbsp Shaoxing wine or
  dry sherry
12 mangetouts (snow peas)
2 spring onions, chopped
coriander (cilantro) leaves, to garnish

Per portion Energy 269kcal/1120kJ; Protein 22g; Carbohydrate 6g, of which sugars 3g; Fat 17g, of which saturates 3g; Cholesterol 53mg; Calcium 49mg; Fibre 0.5g; Sodium 360mg

500g/1¼lb medium prawns (shrimp),
  in their shells
5ml/1 tsp Sichuan peppercorns
30ml/2 tbsp groundnut (peanut) oil
2 garlic cloves, crushed
25g/1oz fresh root ginger, finely grated
4ml/¾ tsp salt
5ml/1 tsp sesame oil
2.5ml/½ tsp caster (superfine) sugar

Variation For a quick version, you can marinate the prawns in the seasonings mixed with the sesame oil and sugar, then drain them thoroughly. Heat the wok with the groundnut oil and add the prawns. Cook for 4–5 minutes, or until pink.

Per portion Energy 124kcal/513kJ; Protein 9g;
Carbohydrate 1g, of which sugars 1g; Fat 9g,
of which saturates 2g; Cholesterol 98mg;
Calcium 43mg; Fibre 0.1g; Sodium 489mg

Prawns in Sichuan pepper sauce

There is nothing quite like cooking prawns in their shells to retain their excellent flavour, and they go very well tossed in a sauce of Sichuan peppercorns. Although most people think of wok cooking as stir-frying, Sichuanese cooks use the wok for many other cooking methods besides this one. Dry-frying is the method used here, called gan pian, in which small pieces of food are stirred vigorously in very little oil until nearly dry.

1 Using kitchen scissors, trim the prawns by snipping off the feelers and the pointed top of the head just behind the eyes. Wash the prawns, drain well and pat very dry with kitchen paper. Put the Sichuan peppercorns in a dry pan and toast for 1 minute. Grind to a powder using a mortar and pestle. Set aside.

2 Heat the oil in a wok over a high heat. When it starts to smoke, add the prawns and fry, stirring vigorously for 1–2 minutes, or until they are only just pink.

3 Add the garlic, ginger and Sichuan pepper, and cook, moving the ingredients backwards and forwards constantly, using a wooden spoon, for 1–2 minutes more, or until the prawns are well coated with the aromatics and cooked through.

4 Add the salt, sesame oil and sugar to the wok and toss together for 15 seconds. The finished prawns should be dry, slightly shiny with oil and speckled with the seasonings. Serve immediately.

Serves 4

1 egg white
2.5ml/$\frac{1}{2}$ tsp salt
450g/1lb raw large prawns (jumbo shrimp) or tiger prawns, shelled
15ml/1 tbsp cornflour (cornstarch)
15ml/1 tbsp groundnut (peanut) oil
2 garlic cloves, crushed
2 spring onions (scallions), cut into 2cm/$\frac{3}{4}$in lengths
40g/1$\frac{1}{2}$oz Hunan or any dry-cured ham, finely diced
50g/2 oz/$\frac{1}{2}$ cup peas, thawed if frozen
10ml/2 tsp Sichuan pepper
30ml/2 tbsp Shaoxing wine or dry sherry
10ml/2 tsp cornflour (cornstarch)
vegetable oil, for deep-frying

Cook's tip If you are using larger prawns, make a deep slit down the back, almost through to the other side. This allows them to cook quickly, and makes them curl up to resemble little blossoms.

Jade prawns Chengdu-style

In this Chengdu dish, quickly fried bright pink prawns contrast with the brilliant green of peas – the jade of the title – cooked with Shaoxing wine and ham. Sichuan cooking reaches its peak in the provincial capital, Chengdu, the centre of the province's culture and cuisine with a history that goes back 2,500 years. With its mild climate and some of Sichuan's best foods, Chengdu's reputation as a culinary capital is well earned.

1 In a large bowl, beat the egg white with salt until almost stiff, then add the prawns and sprinkle over the cornflour. Mix well, then cover and set aside to marinate for 15 minutes.

2 Heat the vegetable oil in a wok over a medium heat or in a deep-fryer. Using a slotted spoon or wire basket, plunge the prawns into the oil for 20 seconds – the prawns should barely sizzle – then drain on kitchen paper.

3 In a clean wok, heat the groundnut oil over a high heat and fry the garlic for 15 seconds. Add the spring onions, ham, peas and prawns with the Sichuan pepper and Shaoxing wine or sherry, and stir-fry vigorously for 1 minute.

4 Put the cornflour in a bowl and gradually blend with 45ml/3 tbsp water, then add to the wok and continue to stir until the juices bubble and thicken. Serve immediately.

Per portion Energy 243kcal/1015kJ; Protein 24g; Carbohydrate 8g, of which sugars 1g; Fat 12g, of which saturates 2g; Cholesterol 219mg; Calcium 104mg; Fibre 0.8g; Sodium 680mg

Wine-marinated prawns

Large prawns are marinated in wine and sugar then quickly fried with leek, green pepper and celery in this delicate dish. Of all the Chinese wines, the Sichuan-brewed wu liang ye (five-grained wine) is best to bring out the richness of the prawns. It is an intensely flavoured liquor made from sorghum grains, glutinous rice, barley, wheat and corn and is a heady 60 per cent proof. However, it is also expensive and not easy to find except in major Chinese supermarkets, so the next best thing is the easily available rose-flavoured wine, mei kuei lu, which comes from northern China.

1 Put the prawns in a bowl and add the wine and sugar. Cover, then leave to marinate in the refrigerator for 20 minutes.

2 Heat the oil in a wok over a high heat. Fry the leek, spring onion, green pepper and celery for 1 minute.

3 Add the prawns and their marinade and stir-fry vigorously for 1 minute, then add the soy sauce and sesame oil. Cook for 1 minute, stirring, then serve immediately.

Serves 4

450g/1lb raw large prawns
  (jumbo shrimp)
45ml/3 tbsp mei kuei lu wine
5ml/1 tsp caster (superfine) sugar
15ml/1 tbsp groundnut (peanut) oil
1 leek, white part only, thinly sliced
1 spring onion (scallion), chopped
1 green (bell) pepper, chopped
1 small celery stick, thinly sliced
15ml/1 tbsp light soy sauce
5ml/1 tsp sesame oil

Cook's tip In Sichuan they don't cook the prawns. The wine in the marinade pickles them, then they are tossed with the fried vegetables.

Per portion Energy 151kcal/632kJ; Protein 20g; Carbohydrate 3g, of which sugars 2g; Fat 6g, of which saturates 1g; Cholesterol 219mg; Calcium 103mg; Fibre 0.6g; Sodium 487mg

Paper-wrapped prawns

Unlike the inedible paper used for a similar Cantonese dish, the paper used for these prawn parcels is completely edible. Sold as 'wafer pastry' in Chinese supermarkets, it is extremely delicate and needs deft and quick handling. The prawns are first seasoned with lime juice and oyster sauce then wrapped in the pastry and immediately fried to make them superbly crisp and light. Sesame oil is added to the vegetable oil to give a tasty nutty fragrance.

1 Make a shallow cut down the centre of the curved back of each prawn. Pull out the black vein with a cocktail stick (toothpick) or your fingers, then rinse the prawn thoroughly and pat dry. Make a deep slit down the underside to open up the prawns and give them a better shape. Put them in a shallow dish.

2 Put the oyster sauce in a small bowl and mix in the lime juice, sugar, pepper and cornflour. Sprinkle this seasoning over the prawns and turn to coat.

3 To make the chilli sauce, grind the chillies in a mortar and pestle or coffee grinder until very fine. Add the vinegar and salt, and stir to mix.

4 Heat the vegetable oil in a wok or deep-fryer, then add the sesame oil. Remove a pastry sheet carefully and place a prawn in the middle. Fold the pastry up, drawing all sides toward the centre and press the edges together to seal in the prawn. This is the same method used for making won tons. Occasionally, the moistness of the marinade might render the pastry a little mushy. When this happens, wrap both the prawn and the paper in an additional paper.

5 Drop the pastry-wrapped prawn into the oil. Remove with a slotted spoon as soon as it turns light brown. The pastry will firm up as it browns in the hot oil; be careful not to let the parcel become scorched. Wrap and cook the remaining prawn parcels as you make them; do not pre-wrap the prawns and leave them to fry in one go, as they will quickly become soggy. Drain on absorbent paper and serve with the chilli dip.

Serves 4

16 tiger prawns (jumbo shrimp), peeled
15ml/1 tbsp oyster sauce
5ml/1 tsp lime juice
5ml/1 tsp caster (superfine) sugar
5ml/1 tsp ground black pepper
15ml/1 tbsp cornflour (cornstarch)
16 or more Chinese wafer pastry sheets
30ml/2 tbsp sesame oil
vegetable oil, for deep-frying

For the chilli dip:
3–4 red chillies, finely chopped
60–75ml4–5 tbsp Kao Liang vinegar
a pinch of salt

Cook's tip If you work quickly and add the prawns to the hot oil immediately, the seasoning won't have a chance to seep through the pastry and make it soggy.

Per portion Energy 288kcal/1214kJ; Protein 10g; Carbohydrate 18g, of which sugars 2g; Fat 20g, of which saturates 3g; Cholesterol 98mg; Calcium 46mg; Fibre 0 g; Sodium 563mg

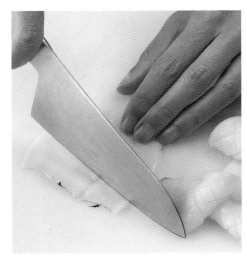

Chilli squid

This member of the vast cephalopod family is an important seafood and is eaten widely in most of coastal China. They can range in size from 2.5cm/1in long to giants of enormous size, but the best size for eating are those about 7.5cm/3in in length, which are available frozen in many Chinese and South-east Asian stores. Squid cooks in moments and is delicious stir-fried in a chilli, garlic and yellow bean sauce.

1 With a sharp knife, slice down the back of the body sac of the squid and flatten out. Score shallow parallel cuts in the flesh, cutting only halfway through. Turn the sac 90° and make another series of cuts to form a grid pattern. Slice into large pieces about 4cm/1½in across. Wash all the cut squid, including the tentacles and wings, then drain. Put the cornflour in a small bowl and gradually blend in 60ml/4 tbsp of cold water. Set aside.

2 Put the chillies and garlic in a mortar and grind to a fine paste using a pestle. Transfer to a small bowl and mix with the yellow bean sauce and sugar. Heat the oil in a wok over a high heat and fry this paste for 45 seconds, or until fragrant.

3 Add the sliced leek and stir-fry for 1 minute, then add the squid and fry for 15 seconds. Stir in the cornflour mixture and cook for 1 minute, or until the squid begins to curl up and the sauce has thickened. Serve, garnished with spring onion, if you like.

Cook's tip

If you buy fresh squid, your fishmonger will prepare it for you but you can also do it yourself, if you like. Hold the squid and pull the tentacles and head free of the body sac. Cut across the tentacles just below the eyes, and discard the eyes and everything above them. Pop out and discard the mouth from inside the tentacles. Cut any longer tentacles into smaller pieces. Slice down the back of the body sac and flatten out. Remove the transparent quill and any fatty, spongy matter.

Serves 4

200g/7oz squid, cleaned, body sac
  left whole (see Cook's Tip)
5ml/1 tsp cornflour (cornstarch)
3 fresh red chillies, seeded and
  roughly chopped
2 garlic cloves, crushed
15ml/1 tbsp yellow bean sauce
5ml/1 tsp caster (superfine) sugar
30ml/2 tbsp groundnut (peanut) oil
½ leek, white part only, thinly
  sliced horizontally
1 chopped spring onion (scallion),
  to garnish (optional)

Per portion Energy 127kcal/529kJ; Protein 8g; Carbohydrate 5g, of which sugars 2g; Fat 8g, of which saturates 2g; Cholesterol 113mg; Calcium 18mg; Fibre 0.4g; Sodium 57mg

Poultry

Chicken lies at the very heart of Chinese cuisine. The humble bird has a unique and versatile flavour, as well as both nutritional and symbolic promise. Likened to the phoenix that rises from the ashes, chicken is a vital component of festive meals. Together with duck, pork and fish, chicken is one of the 'four heroes of the table' in Chinese culinary mythology. Duck is a culinary favourite in western China. It is skilfully transformed into a medley of steamed, braised and fried dishes, some of which have been successfully exported around the world to become global favourites.

Succulent chicken and crispy duck

The Chinese were among the earliest peoples to domesticate fowl and, in some rural farmhouses, you can see an exotic, black-skinned breed of chicken covered by wispy white feathers. Even today, people regard this breed as having special nutritional qualities for new mothers to regain their strength after childbirth.

Many chicken dishes achieve exquisite flavour from the aromatics, wine and chillies that are used in cooking. Spicy chicken dishes such as Kung Po Chicken and Chilli Chicken are perfect examples of supremely tasty western Chinese cooking. Kung Po is attributed to a governor of Sichuan in the late Qing dynasty, Gong Bao. Interestingly, its name had to be changed when it incurred the wrath of Cultural Revolution radicals, but today, you can find Kung Po sauce in supermarkets all over the world!

Another method of cooking chicken is to braise it in rice wine or vinegar. This makes a lovely winter warmer when it is teamed with typical local produce like cloud ears, bamboo pith and even tripe. Hubei chefs are famously fond of using garlic, which they do to an extent that elsewhere might send people scurrying. Shaanxi is known for its method of dry-frying, best manifest in Dry-Fried Hot-and-Sour chicken.

Duck is cooked with pride and a medley of flavourings in western China, and Sichuan is the birthplace of the world-famous and delicious Aromatic Crispy Duck, which has even nudged Peking duck into second place in popularity.

Kung Po chicken

This dish is derived from the name of a late Qing Dynasty official, Ding Baozhen (1820–86), who became Gong Bao, or palatial guardian, and was given the title Kung Pao, or Kung Po. The chicken is cooked with the authentic flavourings of Sichuan peppercorns and fresh, boiled peanuts. Purists would use authentic Sichuan chillies, which are small and fiery, but here we use chilli bean paste, dou banjiang, to give the dish its heat.

1 Cut the chicken into 2.5cm/1in cubes. Put the cornflour in a bowl and blend with the wine or sherry, soy sauce and sesame oil. Add the chicken cubes to this mixture and toss to coat completely. Leave to marinate for 20 minutes.

2 Heat the oil in a wok and stir-fry the garlic and ginger for 40 seconds until golden brown. Add the peppercorns and chilli bean paste, and stir for 30 seconds until well mixed.

3 Add the chicken pieces to the wok and continue to stir over a high heat for 3–4 minutes, or until the chicken is cooked and the sauce is reduced a little – the chicken should be fairly dry but succulent.

4 Stir in the boiled peanuts, sugar and 150ml/¼ pint/⅔ cup water, then continue to stir over a high heat until the mixture comes to the boil. Turn off the heat and serve.

Cook's tips
• Although chilli bean paste (dou banjiang) is characteristic of Sichuan cooking, you can use normal chilli paste or sauce instead, if you like.
• Boiled peanuts are usually available in cans or jars in Chinese supermarkets. Alternatively, you can buy ordinary, shelled raw peanuts in their skins and boil them for 1 hour until soft.

Serves 4

300g/11oz skinless chicken
  breast fillets
15ml/1 tbsp cornflour (cornstarch)
30ml/2 tbsp Shaoxing wine or
  dry sherry
15ml/1 tbsp light soy sauce
15ml/1 tbsp sesame oil
30ml/2 tbsp groundnut (peanut) oil
2 garlic cloves, chopped
30ml/2 tbsp chopped fresh
  root ginger
15ml/1 tbsp Sichuan peppercorns,
  finely crushed
30ml/2 tbsp chilli bean paste
  (dou banjiang)
50g/2oz/⅓ cup boiled peanuts
  (see Cook's Tip)
30ml/2 tbsp soft dark brown sugar

Per portion Energy 286kcal/1194kJ; Protein 21g; Carbohydrate 14g, of which sugars 10g; Fat 16g, of which saturates 3g; Cholesterol 53mg; Calcium 24mg; Fibre 0.7g; Sodium 506mg

Serves 4

450g/1lb boneless chicken thighs
45ml/3 tbsp groundnut (peanut) oil
6 garlic cloves, sliced
15ml/1 tbsp chilli oil (see Cook's Tip)
5ml/1 tsp caster (superfine) sugar
15ml/1 tbsp light soy sauce
2 spring onions (scallions), chopped
boiled rice, to serve

Garlic chicken in Sichuan chilli oil

This rich and fiery dish hails from Hubei and is strongly flavoured with slices of fried garlic. Even with the intense flavour of chilli oil, a product used throughout the western regions of China, the garlic comes through with a vengeance. It is, however, truly scrumptious. Use chicken thighs instead of breast meat for a more succulent flavour. Serve on a bed of rice.

1 Cut the chicken into small dice. Heat the oil in a wok over a medium heat and fry the garlic for 1–2 minutes, or until golden brown. Add the chicken pieces and stir-fry for 2 minutes, or until they turn opaque and are almost cooked through.

2 Add the chilli oil, sugar and soy sauce, then cook, stirring frequently, for 1–2 minutes, or until the chicken is completely cooked.

3 Add 100ml/3½fl oz/scant ½ cup water and the spring onions, then continue to stir-fry until the mixture is nearly dry. Serve with the boiled rice.

Cook's tip Chinese stores sell two types of chilli oil. One that has a ground chilli sediment, and is much like the oil you are offered in Chinese restaurants. This can be slightly acrid. The other is a clear, red chilli oil without any solid chilli matter and is best used here because it is more aromatic and less bitter.

Variation If you like your food hot, some Hunan versions also include a few large dried Sichuan chillies snipped into pieces and added at the same time as the chicken.

Per portion Energy 270kcal/1125kJ; Protein 24g;
Carbohydrate 3g, of which sugars 2g; Fat 18g,
of which saturates 4g; Cholesterol 118mg;
Calcium 16mg; Fibre 0.3g; Sodium 369mg

Chicken with bamboo shoots

This classic dish from Yunnan, the southernmost province of western China, is simple to prepare and uses ingredients that are common throughout China: Chinese celery leaves, chicken, sesame oil and yellow bean sauce, which marry well with the strong flavour of bamboo shoots.

1 Soak the bamboo shoots in cold water for 10 minutes. Meanwhile, slice the chicken into strips about 2cm/³⁄₄in wide. Slice the soaked bamboo shoots into strips or leave as thin slices if they are fairly small.

2 Heat the oil in a wok until you can see the barest hint of smoke curling up, then add the chicken and stir-fry for 1 minute.

3 Add the bamboo shoots and stir-fry for 1 minute. Add the celery leaves and cook, stirring, for 1 minute, then add the sesame oil, yellow bean sauce and sugar, and stir for 1 minute more. Taste and add soy sauce only if the dish requires further salting, as yellow bean sauce is already salty.

4 Put the cornflour in a bowl and gradually blend in 200ml/7fl oz/scant 1 cup water, then pour this into the wok and cook, stirring, for 3 minutes, or until the sauce is thick. Serve hot.

Serves 4

200g/7oz bamboo shoot slices,
  drained and rinsed
450g/1lb skinless chicken breast fillets
30ml/2 tbsp groundnut (peanut) oil
15ml/1 tbsp chopped Chinese
  celery leaves
15ml/1 tbsp sesame oil
15ml/1 tbsp yellow bean sauce
2.5ml/½ tsp caster (superfine) sugar
15ml/1 tbsp light soy sauce, or to taste
5ml/1 tsp cornflour (cornstarch)

Cook's tip
Prepared bamboo shoots can be bought in vacuum packs. Because they never become mushy even when cooked for a long time, bamboo shoots can be added with the chicken.

Per portion Energy 202kcal/847kJ; Protein 28g; Carbohydrate 3g, of which sugars 1g; Fat 9g, of which saturates 2g; Cholesterol 79mg; Calcium 17mg; Fibre 0.9g; Sodium 337mg

Chilli chicken

If Sichuan cooking comes in at 8 on the chilli scale of 1–10, Hunan dishes can top 11! This sister province, while leaning heavily on Sichuan culinary techniques, goes one better when adding the hot pod. Strangely though, this high-octane chicken dish does not scorch the tongue so much as tantalize it – the better to savour the flavour of the whole dish. Most diners do not eat the dried chilli pieces, but you can do so if you want an other-world experience.

1 Cut the chicken into 1cm/½in cubes. Drain the chillies and cut each into two or three pieces.

2 Heat the oil in a wok and fry the chillies for 30 seconds, or until the oil takes on an intense red colour. Remove the chillies using a slotted spoon and set aside. Fry the chicken pieces in the remaining oil for 2 minutes, then remove and drain on kitchen paper.

3 Add the chopped onion and ginger to the wok and fry for 2 minutes, or until golden. Return the chicken to the pan with the spring onions, salt and wine or sherry. Stir-fry for 2 minutes.

4 Return the fried chillies to the pan and continue to stir-fry for 2 minutes. Pour in the sesame oil and stir to mix thoroughly. The dish will have a rich red sauce. Serve immediately.

Variation Instead of chicken, use pork neck fillet or belly trimmed of skin and some of the fat.

Serves 4

450g/1lb skinless chicken breast fillets
5 large dried chillies, soaked and
  seeded (see Cook's Tip)
30ml/2 tbsp groundnut (peanut) oil
½ large onion, finely chopped
25g/1oz fresh root ginger, sliced
2 spring onions (scallions), cut into
  short lengths
2.5ml/½ tsp salt
30ml/2 tbsp Shaoxing wine or
  dry sherry
30ml/2 tbsp sesame oil

Cook's tip The best dried chillies are the largest, each about 7.5cm/3in long and deep burgundy in colour.

Per portion Energy 270kcal/1126kJ; Protein 28g; Carbohydrate 1g, of which sugars 1g; Fat 16g, of which saturates 3g; Cholesterol 79mg; Calcium 19mg; Fibre 0.1g; Sodium 2527mg

Serves 4

2 skinless chicken breast fillets
200ml/7fl oz/scant 1 cup boiling water
30ml/2 tbsp groundnut (peanut) oil
2 garlic cloves, chopped
3 fresh red chillies, seeded and
  chopped, plus 1 fresh red chilli,
  seeded and sliced, to garnish
30ml/2 tbsp sesame oil
50g/2oz/⅓ cup boiled peanuts
  (see Cook's Tip, page 72)
5ml/1 tsp caster (superfine) sugar
5ml/1 tsp cornflour (cornstarch)
1 spring onion (scallion), chopped
boiled rice, to serve

Per portion Energy 285kcal/1185kJ; Protein 18g;
Carbohydrate 5g, of which sugars 3g; Fat 21g,
of which saturates 4g; Cholesterol 44mg;
Calcium 17mg; Fibre 0.9g; Sodium 40mg

Chilli chicken cubes with peanuts

At first glance this Guizhou dish might appear similar to the famous Sichuan Kung Po Chicken. However, this provincial variation has more fire due to its liberal use of fresh chillies, and has fewer aromatics.

1 Cut the chicken into 1cm/½in cubes and put into a pan with the water. Bring to the boil and cook for 6–8 minutes. Lift out the chicken with a slotted spoon and set aside. Leave the stock to cool completely.

2 Heat the oil in a wok and fry the garlic for 40 seconds, or until golden brown. Add the chillies and fry for 1 minute, or until soft. Add the sesame oil, peanuts, chicken and sugar, then stir-fry quickly for 1 minute.

3 Put the cornflour in a bowl and gradually blend with the cold stock. Add this to the wok and cook for 1 minute, or until the sauce thickens, then add the spring onion. Stir to mix well, then immediately remove from the heat. (Alternatively, you can sprinkle over the spring onions as part of the garnish.) Serve with rice, and garnished with the sliced chilli.

Variation Instead of peanuts, you can use cashew nuts or even diced water chestnuts.

Dry-fried hot-and-sour chicken

Shaanxi is perhaps less known for its culinary excellence than for the discovery of those spectacular terracotta soldiers from its capital Xi'an, which was China's former capital. It borrows many of its cooking concepts, such as the dry-frying used here, from its southern neighbour Sichuan and Hubei to the east. The technique of dry-frying uses very little oil or liquid, giving the chicken and vegetables a crisp, almost pickled flavour.

1 Cut the chicken into strips about 2cm/³⁄₄in wide. Heat the oil in a wok and fry the ginger for 1 minute, or until golden brown. Add the chicken, celery, spring onions and chilli bean paste. Stir-fry for 2 minutes over a medium heat.

2 Add the sugar to the wok, then the peppercorns and wine, and continue to stir-fry for a further 2 minutes, or until the chicken is nearly cooked through.

3 Sprinkle 30ml/2 tbsp water over the chicken and cook until the wok is nearly dry and the chicken is cooked through and has a darkish hue from the sauce.

Serves 4

450g/1lb boneless chicken thighs
15ml/1 tbsp groundnut (peanut) oil
25g/1oz fresh root ginger,
   sliced into strips
2 Chinese or English celery
   sticks, sliced
2 spring onions (scallions),
   sliced into short lengths
30ml/2 tbsp chilli bean paste
   (dou banjiang)
2.5ml/¹⁄₂ tsp caster (superfine) sugar
2.5ml/¹⁄₂ tsp Sichuan
   peppercorns, crushed
15ml/1 tbsp rice vinegar
noodles, to serve

Per portion Energy 174kcal/729kJ; Protein 24g; Carbohydrate 4g, of which sugars 3g; Fat 7g, of which saturates 2g; Cholesterol 118mg; Calcium 25mg; Fibre 0.3g; Sodium 308mg

Stir-fried chicken with cloud ears

The contrasting textures of this dish make it especially attractive. Cloud ears have a pleasant crunchy texture and smoky flavour, and Chongqing cooks use them liberally. Chinese chives are thicker, coarser and more pungent than the Western kind, adding to the contrasts in the dish.

1 Cut the chicken into cubes. Trim off any tough parts from the cloud ears, then rinse and drain them. Slice the larger pieces into two. Set aside.

2 Heat the oil in a wok and fry the chives and ginger for 2 minutes, or until light brown. Add the chicken and cloud ears to the wok and stir-fry for 3 minutes.

3 Add the sesame oil, yellow bean sauce and sugar, and stir-fry for 2 minutes. Put the cornflour in a bowl and gradually blend in 100ml/3½ fl oz/scant ½ cup water. Pour into the sauce and stir until it thickens. Serve with boiled rice.

Cook's tip Cloud ears are also known as tree ears (mu erh), as they resemble a human ear in shape. They are wild mushrooms, parasitic fungi that grow on tree trunks, and are thin and brittle. When soaked in water they swell up to resemble frilly clumps of rubbery seaweed.

Variation Ordinary Chinese mushrooms can be used instead of cloud ears, but they won't have the characteristic crunch and texture.

Serves 4

450g/1lb skinless chicken breast fillets
5g/⅛oz cloud ear (wood ear)
  mushrooms, soaked in warm water
  for 10–15 minutes
30ml/2 tbsp groundnut (peanut) oil
2 stalks Chinese chives, chopped
20g/¾oz fresh root ginger, shredded
30ml/2 tbsp sesame oil
15ml/1 tbsp yellow bean sauce
2.5ml/½ tsp caster (superfine) sugar
5ml/1 tsp cornflour (cornstarch)
boiled rice, to serve

Per portion Energy 271kcal/1131kJ; Protein 27g;
Carbohydrate 4g, of which sugars 1g; Fat 16g,
of which saturates 3g; Cholesterol 79mg;
Calcium 13mg; Fibre 0.1g; Sodium 69mg

Chicken in vinegar sauce

This tart and aromatic dish from Chongqing is steeped in a rich vinegar sauce, which has a great affinity with bamboo shoots. Chongqing, a municipality bordering Sichuan, has a cuisine that is generally regarded as being distinct from its famous neighbour, and certainly not representative of orthodox western Chinese cooking. This dish, however, has fragrant echoes of the classic Sichuan style, especially in its use of spicy chillies.

1 Put the egg white in a bowl and whisk until almost stiff. Cut the chicken into thin pieces, about 4cm/1½in square and 5mm/¼in thick. Put the salt and wine or sherry into the bowl with the egg white, then add the chicken and toss to coat evenly. Leave to marinate for 15 minutes.

2 Cut the chillies in half and remove the seeds, then cut them into small dice. Heat the oil in a wok and fry the chillies for 30 seconds – be careful not to scorch them.

3 Add the chicken and its marinade to the wok, then add the bamboo shoots. Stir-fry for 1 minute.

4 To make the vinegar sauce, put the cornflour in a small bowl and gradually blend in the remaining sauce ingredients and 45ml/3 tbsp water. When well combined, add to the wok.

5 Cook, stirring frequently, for 2–3 minutes, or until the sauce thickens and the chicken is cooked through. Serve with boiled rice.

Variation The bamboo shoots can be replaced with sliced leeks for an even more pungent flavour, if you like.

Serves 4

1 egg white
2 skinless chicken breast fillets, about 300g/11oz in total
5ml/1 tsp salt
30ml/2 tbsp Shaoxing wine or dry sherry
2 dried chillies, soaked until soft
15ml/1 tbsp groundnut (peanut) oil
90g/3½oz bamboo shoot strips
boiled rice, to serve

For the vinegar sauce
5ml/1 tsp cornflour (cornstarch)
15ml/1 tbsp rice vinegar
15ml/1 tbsp light soy sauce
5ml/1 tsp caster (superfine) sugar
5ml/1 tsp finely grated ginger
1 garlic clove, crushed
1 spring onion (scallion) white part only, very finely chopped

Per portion Energy 143kcal/599kJ; Protein 19g; Carbohydrate 4g, of which sugars 2g; Fat 5g, of which saturates 1g; Cholesterol 53mg; Calcium 13mg; Fibre 0.5g; Sodium 822mg

Wine-braised chicken

Cantonese rice wine, or mi jiu, which is a pale, light alcohol, makes a good marinade for the chicken in this dish, combined with the flavours of celery, garlic and ginger. In general, Chinese chefs are not overly fussy about the brands of wine they use as long as they are not grape wines, which they consider unsuitable for their cooking needs.

1 Cut the chicken into 2.5cm/1in cubes. Put the rice wine in a bowl and blend in the garlic, ginger, pepper, sugar and salt. Stir in the chicken to coat evenly and leave to marinate for 15 minutes.

2 Heat the oil in a wok over a high heat. Fry the celery for 30 seconds, then reduce the heat slightly and add the chicken and its marinade. Stir-fry for 2 minutes, or until the chicken is barely cooked and the juices have reduced slightly.

3 Stir in the soy sauce and sesame oil. Put the cornflour in a bowl and gradually blend in 200ml/7fl oz/scant 1 cup water. Stir into the wok mixture, then simmer for 1 minute, or until the sauce bubbles and thickens. Garnish with chopped celery leaves and serve with noodles.

Cook's tip If you really can't find any good rice wine, use a medium-dry sherry.

Variation A less tender cut of chicken, such as thigh meat, can be used instead of chicken breast fillets, if you like. The marinade will tenderize them.

Serves 4

450g/1lb skinless chicken breast fillets
45ml/3 tbsp Chinese rice wine or
  medium-dry sherry
30ml/2 tbsp crushed garlic
  (4–5 cloves)
30ml/2 tbsp grated fresh root ginger
2.5ml/½ tsp white pepper
2.5ml/½ tsp caster (superfine) sugar
2.5ml/½ tsp salt
30ml/2 tbsp groundnut (peanut) oil
1 celery stick, sliced
15ml/1 tbsp light soy sauce
5ml/1 tsp sesame oil
5ml/1 tsp cornflour (cornstarch)
200ml/7fl oz/scant 1 cup water
chopped Chinese celery leaves,
  to garnish
egg noodles, to serve

Per portion Energy 231kcal/967J; Protein 28g; Carbohydrate 5g, of which sugars 2g; Fat 10g, of which saturates 2g; Cholesterol 79mg; Calcium 13mg; Fibre 0.4g; Sodium 344mg

Serves 4

1 chicken, about 1.6kg/3½lb,
  or 8 chicken portions
250g/9oz prepared tripe
30ml/2 tbsp groundnut (peanut) oil
3 garlic cloves, crushed
25g/1oz fresh root ginger, sliced
½ large onion, sliced
30ml/2 tbsp Shaoxing wine or
  dry sherry
15ml/1 tbsp light soy sauce
30ml/2 tbsp oyster sauce
15ml/1 tbsp sesame oil
2.5ml/½ tsp ground black pepper
800ml/27fl oz/scant 3¼ cups water
coriander (cilantro) leaves, to garnish

Per portion Energy 414kcal/1723kJ; Protein35g;
Carbohydrate 3g, of which sugars 1g; Fat 28g,
of which saturates 7g; Cholesterol 174mg;
Calcium 63mg; Fibre 0.1g; Sodium 695mg

Braised chicken with tripe

Although tripe may seem like an unusual ingredient, chefs in the province of Yunnan are adept at combining the most unlikely ingredients and making them work brilliantly. Tripe is included in their cuisine as much for its texture as for its taste, and here it is combined with chicken and aromatic seasonings and sauces. The dish is traditionally cooked with a whole chicken on the bone, but using joints cuts the cooking time.

1 If using a whole chicken, joint it into eight or more pieces. Removing any excess fat and gristle from the joints or chicken portions. Wash and slice the tripe into small pieces, each about 5cm/2in long x 2.5cm/1in wide.

2 Heat the oil in a wok and fry the garlic, ginger and onion for 1 minute. Add the chicken and tripe, and stir-fry for 2 minutes.

3 Add the wine or sherry to the wok with the soy sauce, oyster sauce, sesame oil and pepper. Cook, stirring, for 2 minutes over a high heat.

4 Add 800ml/1½ pints/scant 3¼ cups water, then bring to the boil and simmer, covered, for 40 minutes, or until all the meat is tender. Serve immediately, garnished with coriander.

Aromatic crispy duck

Of all Sichuan exports, this dish has earned its place in the global culinary hall of fame. Five-spice powder, Sichuan peppercorns, garlic and ginger give the duck its wonderful aroma. It is first steamed in the aromatics, then left to absorb all the flavours before being quickly fried. It is sometimes confused with Peking Duck, but is prepared in a completely different way. Although it requires more work than its Peking cousin, it is well worth the effort.

1 Clean the duck inside and out, and pat dry. Cut down the breastbone, then open the bird out and press it flat to spatchcock it. Remove any excess fat pads. Put the salt in a small bowl and add the garlic, ginger and spring onions. Stir in the rice wine or vinegar, five-spice powder and peppercorns. Rub this all over the duck, pressing on the aromatics.

2 Put the duck on a tray or in a large bowl and place over a wok or steamer containing simmering water. Steam over a high heat for 1½–2 hours, or until completely tender but not collapsed. Take the tray or bowl out of the wok and leave the duck to infuse (steep) in its juices for 1 hour. Drain and place on a rack. (Save the juices for a soup or stock.)

3 Remove all the aromatics from the duck, and leave it to stand for a while until the skin is dry. Meanwhile, prepare the accompaniments: put the pancakes in a steamer, put the spring onions, cucumber and hoisin sauce in separate small dishes, and transfer to the table.

4 With a pastry brush, dust the duck lightly all over with cornflour or water chestnut flour. Heat the vegetable oil in a wok over a medium heat or in a deep-fryer. Carefully lower the duck into the oil (a wide Chinese mesh strainer is perfect for this) and deep-fry until crisp and golden, turning and basting the duck with oil during frying. If your wok is too small, cut the duck into quarters and fry a piece at a time. Lift out the duck and drain on kitchen paper.

5 Transfer the duck to a serving plate and use a knife and fork to shred the crisp skin and meat into strips, removing the bones as you go. Steam the pancakes in a steamer set over simmering water for 3 minutes, until hot, then take to the table. Each diner spreads a little hoisin sauce on a pancake, then tops it with a few strips of spring onion and cucumber, and some shredded duck. Then the diner will roll up the pancake and eat.

Serves 8–10

1 oven-ready duck, about 2.5kg/5½lb
5ml/1 tsp salt
4 garlic cloves, crushed
25g/1oz fresh root ginger,
 finely grated
3 spring onions (scallions),
 cut into 5cm/2in lengths
45ml/3 tbsp rice wine or vinegar
5ml/1 tsp five-spice powder
5ml/1 tsp Sichuan peppercorns,
 lightly crushed
30–45ml/2–3 tbsp cornflour
 (cornstarch) or water chestnut flour
vegetable oil, for deep-frying

For the accompaniments
24–30 Mandarin pancakes
spring onions (scallions), sliced into
 thin strips
cucumber, sliced into thin batons
hoisin sauce

Cook's tip
You can wave a hairdryer over the duck after steaming it at step 3, to help the skin dry out, if you like.

Per portion Energy 602kcal/2491kJ; Protein 20g; Carbohydrate 5g, of which sugars 0g; Fat 64g, of which saturates 16g; Cholesterol 108mg; Calcium 22mg; Fibre 0.1g; Sodium 301mg

Duck with bamboo piths

Bamboo piths have a wonderful crunchy texture and robust taste, and are cooked in many dishes from Hubei and Sichuan. Here they are partnered with Chinese dried sweet dates for their fruitiness. Unlike natural dates, they are caramelized with sugar and go well with rich duck meat.

1 If you are using duck legs, remove the bones by making deep slits along the thickest part and, with a sharp paring knife, carefully scraping the meat away from the bone. Twist the bone and take it out – it should come out easily. Cut each leg into three or four pieces. If you are using duck breast fillets, remove the skin if you prefer, then slice each into three or four pieces. Wash and pat dry.

2 Heat the oil in a wok and fry the garlic and ginger for 1 minute. Add the duck pieces and stir-fry for 2 minutes, or until well sealed. Add the soy sauce and yellow bean sauce, then cook the sauce, stirring frequently, for 2 minutes.

3 Add the tangerine peel, dates, sugar and 600ml/1 pint/2½ cups water, then cook, stirring occasionally, over a high heat for 3 minutes, or until the sauce is reduced by half and thickens. Cut the bamboo piths into small pieces and add to the wok.

4 Reduce the heat to low and simmer for 5–8 minutes, or until the duck is tender. Serve immediately, garnished with shredded spring onions.

Cook's tips
• Bamboo piths are always sold in dried form and look like skeins of shrivelled silk with a dark tan colour. They are sometimes sold as bamboo pith fungus or simply bamboo fungus. Soak the piths in warm water for about 20 minutes before cooking them. If you cannot find them, you can use ordinary bamboo shoots instead.
• Chinese dried dates come in two forms: natural or caramelized with sugar, called mat cho in Cantonese. The caramelized dates are recommended for this dish. If you cannot find Chinese sweet dates, you can use Middle Eastern sweet dates instead.

Serves 4

4 duck legs or 2 duck breast fillets
30ml/2 tbsp groundnut (peanut) oil
3 garlic cloves, crushed
25g/1oz fresh root ginger, chopped
30ml/2 tbsp dark soy sauce
15ml/1 tbsp yellow bean sauce
1 small piece of tangerine peel, about 5cm/2in square
10 Chinese dried sweet dates, pitted
5ml/1 tsp caster (superfine) sugar
75g/3oz bamboo piths, soaked until soft (see Cook's Tip)
noodles, to serve
shredded spring onions (scallions), to garnish

Per portion Energy 287kcal/1207kJ; Protein 17g; Carbohydrate 28g, of which sugars 26g; Fat 13g, of which saturates 3g; Cholesterol 83mg; Calcium 34mg; Fibre 1.9g; Sodium 517mg

Braised duck with tofu

As a winter warmer this dish is very comforting, with its wine sauce and blended seasonings that bring out the flavour of the duck. While fruity sauces like plum really cut the fat of duck, aromatics like garlic and ginger also do the same job. Tofu pieces with their firm outside and soft centre provide the perfect contrast. Although typical of Sichuan, it is by no means exclusive to this province – Hubei and Hunan have their own versions. If you can find French duck breasts, they are ideal for this dish as they have more lean meat in relation to fatty skin. However, in most Chinese dishes, poultry skin is an important part of the dish, providing flavour and succulence.

1 Cut the duck breasts into slices about 5mm/¼in thick. Cut the tofu into 2cm/¾in cubes.

2 Heat the oil in a wok until smoking hot and fry the tofu cubes until a brown skin forms on all sides. Remove with a slotted spoon and drain on kitchen paper. Set aside. Add the duck pieces to the wok and fry in the remaining oil over a high heat for 2 minutes. Remove with a slotted spoon and drain on kitchen paper.

3 Pour out all but 15ml/1 tbsp of the oil and fry the ginger, garlic and onion for 1 minute, or until nearly brown. Add the hoisin sauce, oyster sauce, wine or sherry and 600ml/1 pint/2½ cups water, then bring to the boil.

4 Return the duck to the wok and braise over a high heat for 2 minutes, or until the sauce is thick and slightly glossy. Add the tofu and cook for a further 3 minutes. Serve with slices of pickled ginger to taste. These come in thin slices in jars or vacuum-packed.

Serves 6–8

2 duck breast fillets
250g/9oz packet firm tofu
75ml/5 tbsp groundnut (peanut) oil
25oz/1 oz fresh root ginger, finely grated
4 garlic cloves, crushed
1 large onion, sliced
30ml/2 tbsp hoisin sauce
15ml/1 tbsp oyster sauce
30ml/2 tbsp Chinese wine or dry sherry
pickled ginger

Cook's tip There is another type of tofu called tofu gan, or firm dried squares, which does not need to be fried as it already has a firm skin. Use this cut into cubes as above and add it for the last 5 minutes of cooking.

Per portion Energy 179kcal/743kJ; Protein 11g; Carbohydrate 4g, of which sugars 2g; Fat 13g, of which saturates 3g; Cholesterol 41mg; Calcium 174mg; Fibre 0.5g; Sodium 179mg

Meat

Although the occasional lamb or game dish appears on menus, pork rules the culinary realm, appearing in myriad guises. Pig-rearing is popular in China as pigs do not need grazing land and are happy in small sties: a family could keep a few in their backyard barns with no trouble at all. The recipe dictates the way the pork is cut, and western Chinese chefs are particular about the ratio of meat to fat in pork. Historically, the cow was not eaten due to its role in the farming industry, which had no mechanical ploughs. Today, however, urban cooks make use of beef in many contemporary recipes.

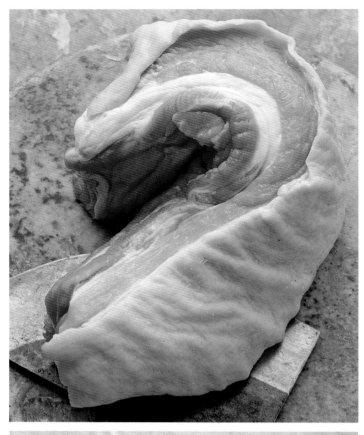

Sticky, crispy and tender meats

Pork, when it is on the menu, comes with specific requirements in western Chinese cooking. Roast pork has to be made from a rib cut that is streaked with the requisite amount of fat, as well as being cut in a wide, long strip. When pork is needed for long cooking or braising, usually the hock or leg cut is used. There is a specific ratio of lean meat to fat and skin that is adhered to by local cooks. This works out at eight parts lean to two parts fat and skin, which results in superb flavour, succulence and texture. This is typified in Twice Cooked Pork, where the pork skin is left on for extra texture, artfully cooked to a crunchy tenderness.

Beef is made into an imperial offering in the iconic Sichuan dish Crispy Chilli Beef, which is now a top-class dish in restaurants across the world. It gets a fiery kick from chilli bean paste, as does Boiled Fiery Beef, which also benefits from the additional heat of dried chillies. Some of these meat dishes are tongue-searingly hot from a liberal blend of two of the region's most potent ingredients – chillies and Sichuan peppercorns. Red-cooked Beef (hong shau) is another piquant favourite, where beef is liberally soused with blends of fermented red bean curd and hoisin sauce.

Western Chinese cooking makes good use of offal, too, elevating it to great heights, such as in the tasty Hot-and-sour Kidneys. Although not very common, the odd game recipe, such as Rabbit in Hot Bean Sauce, demonstrates the exceptional skills of Sichuan chefs.

Cold garlic pork

Pork and garlic go very well together, and are a tasty combination in this cold dish. This Sichuan classic is popular in summer when temperatures and humidity in this province can be unyieldingly oppressive. Sichuan chefs use a special local soy sauce with nuances of sugar and spice for this dish, but this product is rare outside the region, so this recipe uses a light soy sauce tweaked with a little sugar and chilli oil for the best flavour.

1 Put the pork in a large pan and add boiling water to cover. Boil over a high heat for 30 seconds, then remove the pork, put it into a colander and quickly cool with cold water.

2 Put the pork in a large pan and add 1.5 litres/2½ pints/6¼ cups water, the ginger and spring onions. Cover and bring to the boil, then reduce the heat to maintain a gentle simmer and cook, partially covered, for 45–55 minutes, or until the pork is just cooked through and tender.

3 Remove the pan from the heat and allow the pork to cool completely in the cooking liquid, then cover and transfer to the fridge. Leave to chill for at least 2 hours.

4 To make the sauce, put the garlic in a mortar and crush to a paste with a pestle. Transfer to a small bowl and stir in the remaining ingredients. Cover and leave to stand for 15 minutes.

5 When you are ready to serve, slice the pork thinly with a sharp knife. Arrange the slices on a serving platter, fanning them out and overlapping them slightly. Pour the sauce over and serve with pickled ginger.

Serves 4

450g/1lb well-marbled pork shoulder
25g/1oz fresh root ginger, bruised
2 spring onions (scallions)
pickled ginger slices, to serve

For the sauce
6–7 garlic cloves, grated
45ml/3 tbsp light soy sauce
5ml/1 tsp caster (superfine) sugar
15ml/1 tbsp sesame oil
15ml/1 tbsp chilli oil

Per portion Energy 223kcal/933kJ; Protein 24g; Carbohydrate 4g, of which sugars 3g; Fat 12g, of which saturates 3g; Cholesterol 72mg; Calcium 18mg; Fibre 0.3g; Sodium 885mg

Pork ribs in peppercorn sauce

Ribs are given a hot and spicy marinade before being steamed in this dish from Hunan. In some local restaurants the recipe is also adapted to use carp as well as pork ribs, reflecting the cooks' skills at combining two distinctly different flavours in a most innovative way. However, pork ribs on their own are wonderfully succulent and savoury. This dish is perfect served as a first course.

1 Cut the pork ribs into short lengths, about 2.5cm/1in. Bring a large pan of water to the boil and add the spring onions and Sichuan peppercorns. Put the ribs into the pan and bring back to the boil. Simmer for 30 minutes. Remove the pan from the heat and leave the pork in the liquor for 15 minutes to absorb the flavours.

2 Place a dish inside a steamer. Remove the pork ribs with a slotted spoon and put them into the dish. In a small bowl, mix together the ginger, chillies, sugar, ground peppercorns, sesame oil and wine or sherry, then pour this mixture over the pork and toss to coat. Leave to marinate for 20 minutes.

3 Cover the steamer and transfer it to a wok filled with simmering water. Steam for 30 minutes, then serve.

Cook's tip Try to buy your pork ribs from a Chinese butcher if you can, as they are cut to a perfect ratio of bone and meat, unlike the supermarket ribs, which are mostly bone.

Serves 4

450g/1lb pork ribs
3 spring onions (scallions)
5ml/1 tsp whole Sichuan peppercorns
25g/1oz ground ginger
3 fresh red chillies, seeded and
  sliced into strips
5ml/1 tsp caster (superfine) sugar
2.5ml/½ tsp ground
  Sichuan peppercorns
30ml/2 tbsp sesame oil
30ml/2 tbsp Shaoxing wine or
  dry sherry

Per portion Energy 321kcal/1767kJ; Protein 23g; Carbohydrate 7g, of which sugars 6g; Fat 34g, of which saturates 10g; Cholesterol 80mg; Calcium 21mg; Fibre 1.3g; Sodium 634mg

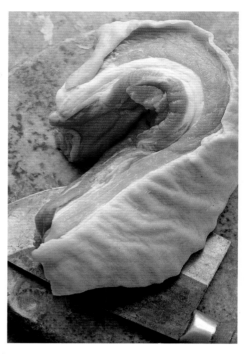

Twice-cooked pork

A Sichuan all-time favourite, the name of this dish is fairly self-explanatory. It is simply pork that is parboiled and then stir-fried with a blend of Sichuan seasonings. This is a very old method of cooking from when tough meats, such as mutton and wild boar, had to be made tender to eat by precooking.

1 Cut the pork into two pieces, then put in a colander over the sink and rinse both sides with boiling water. Drain well. Put the pork in a large pan and cover completely with boiling water. Bring to the boil over a medium heat, then simmer for 30–40 minutes, or until cooked through.

2 Drain (reserve the cooking liquid for a soup or stock) and leave to cool completely, then wrap tightly in clear film (plastic wrap) and chill for 2 hours, or until firm.

3 Using a sharp knife, thinly slice the pork crossways into strips as thin as a bacon rasher (strip) – each piece should be edged with some fat and skin. Cut the leek diagonally into 5mm/¼in thick slices. Cut the pepper into 2.5cm/1in pieces.

4 Heat the oil in a wok over a high heat. Add the pork slices, sugar and soy sauces, and fry vigorously for about 2 minutes, or until the pork is lightly browned and caramelized.

5 Add the garlic, leek and pepper, and stir-fry for 30 seconds, then push all the ingredients to the edge of the wok. Add the hoisin sauce and chilli bean paste to the centre of the wok and fry for several seconds until fragrant, then mix everything together and fry for 1 minute more. Serve immediately, on a bed of noodles, if you like.

Serves 4

450g/1lb meaty pork belly, or pork
    leg with skin and fat
1 small leek
1 green (bell) pepper
45ml/3 tbsp vegetable oil
10ml/2 tsp caster (superfine) sugar
15ml/1 tbsp dark soy sauce
15ml/1 tbsp light soy sauce
2 garlic cloves, chopped
15ml/1 tbsp hoisin sauce
30ml/2 tbsp chilli bean paste
    (dou banjiang)
noodles, to serve (optional)

Cook's tip If you like, you can add 15ml/1 tbsp Chinese wine with the chilli bean paste for a richer flavour.

Per portion Energy 426kcal/1866kJ; Protein 24g; Carbohydrate 20g, of which sugars 4g; Fat 31g, of which saturates 9g; Cholesterol 71mg; Calcium 106mg; Fibre 4.5g; Sodium 507mg

Pork in hot-and-sour sauce

The province of Shaanxi may not enjoy the same exalted culinary status as Sichuan or Hunan, but nonetheless it has some excellent signature dishes. This one is a spicy take on the well-known sweet-and-sour sauce, with a unique flavour from the blend of rice wine or vinegar, chillies and plum sauce, as well as some depth from the aromatics of onion and garlic. Be generous with the fiery flavours, as these are what make the dish.

1 Cut the pork into 2cm/¾in cubes and put into a bowl. Pour over the egg and toss the pork to mix. Put the tapioca flour in a plastic food bag. Lift out the pork using a slotted spoon and allow the excess egg to drain off, then put the pork pieces into the bag. Hold the top of the bag closed and shake the bag to coat the pork in the flour. Take out the pork and shake off the excess flour. Leave on a plate for 15 minutes.

2 Heat the vegetable oil in a wok or deep-fryer and fry the pork, in batches if necessary, until golden brown and crisp. Drain on kitchen paper and keep warm.

3 To make the sauce, mix the rice wine or vinegar with the plum sauce and 45ml/3 tbsp water. Heat the oil in a wok and fry the onion and garlic for 2 minutes, or until light brown. Add the chillies and plum sauce mixture, then bring to a rapid boil. Remove the wok from the heat and toss the pork in the sauce to mix well. Serve on a bed of lettuce.

Cook's tip Chinese chefs rarely, or never, use a wet batter on meats, as it tends to go soft very quickly. With dry batters the meat stays crisp for much longer.

Serves 4

450g/1lb pork rib steak or leg of pork
1 egg, lightly beaten
45ml/3 tbsp tapioca flour
vegetable oil, for deep-frying
lettuce leaves, to serve

For the sauce
30ml/2 tbsp rice wine or vinegar
30ml/2 tbsp plum sauce
30ml/2 tbsp groundnut (peanut) oil
1 medium onion, thinly sliced
3 garlic cloves, thinly sliced
3 fresh red chillies, seeded and chopped

Per portion Energy 327kcal/1364kJ; Protein 27g; Carbohydrate 17g, of which sugars 5g; Fat 17g, of which saturates 3g; Cholesterol 130mg; Calcium 28mg; Fibre 0.7g; Sodium 109mg

Cold spicy beef

Although cold food is not a great favourite among most Chinese, when summers dawn with unrelenting heat – especially in land-locked areas like Sichuan, Hunan and Hubei – this spicy beef dish makes a welcome change. It has overtones of Cantonese-style cold banquet dishes, probably adopted over many decades of migratory movements between the neighbouring provinces. It also uses a uniquely Chinese product, red rice wine lees, the residue of wine made from rice and a special strain of yeast that produces a vivid scarlet colour. If this is unavailable, use red fermented tofu (tofu ru).

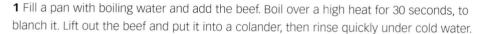

1 Fill a pan with boiling water and add the beef. Boil over a high heat for 30 seconds, to blanch it. Lift out the beef and put it into a colander, then rinse quickly under cold water.

2 Put 1.5 litres/2½ pints/6¼ cups water in the clean pan and add the rice wine or vinegar, red wine lees or fermented tofu, spices, soy sauce and sugar. Add the beef. Cover and bring to the boil, then reduce to a simmer. Cook, partially covered, for 1½ hours, until the beef is tender.

3 Remove the pan from the heat and allow the beef to cool completely in its cooking liquid.

4 Lift out the beef, wrap tightly in clear film (plastic wrap), then chill for 15 minutes to firm it. Meanwhile, make the sauce by mixing all the ingredients together in a small jug (pitcher).

5 Slice the beef very thinly using a sharp knife, and arrange the slices on a serving platter. Drizzle with the sauce and serve immediately.

Serves 4

450g/1lb rump (round) or rib-eye beef, in one piece
15ml/1 tbsp rice wine or vinegar
15ml/1 tbsp red rice wine lees or red fermented tofu (tofu ru)
5ml/1 tsp Sichuan peppercorns
6 cloves
1 stick cinnamon, about 5cm/2in
1 star anise
30ml/2 tbsp light soy sauce
5ml/1 tsp caster (superfine) sugar

For the sauce
2 garlic cloves, crushed
15ml/1 tbsp finely grated ginger
15ml/1 tbsp sesame oil
5ml/1 tsp salt

Per portion Energy 160kcal/672kJ; Protein 25g; Carbohydrate 3g, of which sugars 2g; Fat 5g, of which saturates 2g; Cholesterol 66mg; Calcium 16mg; Fibre 0.1g; Sodium 1096mg

Serves 4

450g/1lb beef fillet
15ml/1 tbsp groundnut (peanut) oil
2 garlic cloves, sliced
15ml/1 tbsp dark soy sauce
5ml/1 tsp caster (superfine) sugar
pinch of ground cloves
2.5ml/½ tsp ground
  Sichuan peppercorns
15ml/1 tbsp sesame oil
150ml/¼ pint/⅔ cup water
15ml/1 tbsp sesame seeds
noodles, to serve

For the marinade
15ml/1 tbsp finely grated ginger
1 spring onion (scallion), finely chopped
2.5ml/½ tsp salt
15ml/1 tbsp rice wine or vinegar

Per portion Energy 255kcal/1062kJ; Protein 25g;
Carbohydrate 2g, of which sugars 2g; Fat 16g,
of which saturates 5g; Cholesterol 69mg;
Calcium 33mg; Fibre 0.3g; Sodium 512mg

Sesame beef

This marinated beef dish originated from Hubei, although it is more usually cooked there using pork. However, there is a sizeable population of Muslims in western China, and this dish was tweaked to suit their religious needs. Known as the Hui people, these Muslims were from the Xinjiang Uighur region before they emigrated to the western provinces. Their modification of the area's pork dishes has given great variation to the local menu.

1 Using a sharp knife, cut the beef into thin slices, each measuring 2.5cm/1in wide by 7.5cm/3in long. Put the marinade ingredients in a bowl and mix well. Pour over the beef and toss to coat evenly. Leave to marinate for 20 minutes.

2 Heat the oil in a wok and fry the sliced garlic until crisp and light brown. Add the beef slices with their marinade and stir-fry for 1 minute.

3 Add the soy sauce, sugar, ground cloves, Sichuan peppercorns and sesame oil, and stir-fry for 1 minute over a high heat.

4 Add 150ml/¼ pint/⅔ cup water and stir until the sauce is reduced by half and the beef is fairly dry and glossy. Serve with noodles, and sprinkled with sesame seeds.

Cook's tip Sesame seeds take on a deliciously nutty fragrance when lightly toasted. To do this, put them in a dry pan over a high heat and toast, shaking the pan regularly, until a light golden brown.

Crispy chilli beef

A restaurant-starred dish, crispy chilli beef has earned legions of fans around the world. Although it is considered to be a Sichuan invention, it has nevertheless been adopted by other regional cuisines, and some Hong Kong chefs have even claimed that it came from their kitchens. It is actually possible that this dish originated from anywhere in China, as imperial courts were forever poaching ideas from other regions. Wherever it first originated, it is certainly a very delicious mouthful. Serve it with boiled rice, if you like.

1 Cut the beef into thin strips about 6cm/2½in long by 1cm/½in wide. Put the strips into a shallow dish. In a small bowl, mix together the marinade ingredients, then pour over the beef and stir to coat evenly. Cover and leave to marinate for 20 minutes. (Marinating will keep the steak juicy.)

2 Heat the vegetable oil in a wok or deep-fryer. Sprinkle the cornflour over the beef and toss to coat, then deep-fry the meat in batches until golden and crispy, stirring with chopsticks to keep the strips separate. Drain on kitchen paper and keep warm. Deep-fry the carrot strips for 15 seconds and drain well.

3 Heat the groundnut oil in a clean wok over a high heat, then fry the garlic for 10 seconds. Add the celery and fry for 20 seconds more.

4 Add the beef, carrot and chilli bean paste, with the hoisin sauce, sesame oil, sugar and salt. Sir-fry vigorously for 1 minute, or until everything is coated with a glossy glaze. Serve immediately, with rice, if you like.

Serves 4

450g/1lb rump (round) or
  rib-eye steak
vegetable oil, for deep-frying
45ml/3 tbsp cornflour (cornstarch)
90g/3½oz carrot, cut into thin strips
30ml/2 tbsp groundnut (peanut) oil
2 garlic cloves, finely chopped
1 celery stick, cut into thin strips
30ml/2 tbsp chilli bean paste
  (dou banjiang)
15ml/1 tbsp hoisin sauce
2.5ml/½ tsp sesame oil
10ml/2 tsp caster (superfine) sugar
2.5ml/½ tsp salt
rice, to serve (optional)

For the marinade
15ml/1 tbsp rice wine or vinegar
1.5ml/¼ tsp salt
1.5ml/¼ tsp caster (superfine) sugar

Per portion Energy 353kcal/1472kJ; Protein 25g; Carbohydrate 18g, of which sugars 7g; Fat 20g, of which saturates 4g; Cholesterol 66mg; Calcium 19mg; Fibre 0.7g; Sodium 500mg

Serves 4

675g/1½lb stewing steak
30ml/2 tbsp vegetable oil
25g/1oz fresh root ginger, sliced
3 garlic cloves, sliced
30ml/2 tbsp chilli bean paste
  (dou banjiang)
30ml/2 tbsp hoisin sauce
5ml/1 tsp Sichuan peppercorns
75ml/5 tbsp rice wine or vinegar
1 mooli (daikon)
salt and ground black pepper
rice, to serve (optional)

Variation You can add any firm vegetables for the last 10 minutes of cooking time (20 minutes for carrots).

Red-cooked beef

The method of braising known as 'red cooking' is not exclusive to Sichuan. It is a technique used in many regions, and various ingredients are used to achieve the characteristic red colouring. Cantonese chefs invariably use a blend of fermented red tofu and hoisin sauce. In Shanghai and Suzhou in the eastern provinces, red wine lees gives the braise an intense colour and alcoholic flavour. Here, both chilli bean paste and hoisin give the dish a hot-sweet finish. Whichever is used, it is the method of slow braising that gives the meat its flavour and texture. Serve with plain rice.

1 Cut the beef into large chunks, about 4cm/1½in. Bring a large pan of water to the boil, add the beef and boil it for 1 minute to blanch it. Lift it out with a slotted spoon and drain on kitchen paper. (Doing this helps to eliminate scum and debris in the braising pan later.)

2 Heat the oil in a large, heavy pan over a medium heat. Add the ginger and garlic, and fry for 1–2 minutes, or until fragrant. Add the chilli bean paste and fry for 30 seconds, then add the hoisin sauce, Sichuan peppercorns, 1 litre/1¾ pints/4 cups water and the rice wine or vinegar. Add the beef, then cover and simmer for 1½ hours, or until the beef is tender.

3 Peel the mooli and cut horizontally into slices about 2.5cm/1in thick. Quarter each slice, or halve smaller slices. Add to the pan and partially cover, then cook for 30 minutes more, or until the mooli is translucent and tender, and the beef is very tender. Adjust the seasoning with salt or pepper to taste. Serve immediately.

Per portion Energy 295kcal/1234kJ; Protein 39g; Carbohydrate 5g, of which sugars 3g; Fat 14g, of which saturates 3g; Cholesterol 113mg; Calcium 26mg; Fibre 0.1g; Sodium 367mg

Five-spice beef in bean sauce

The famous blend of five spices is universally used in China, and Sichuan is no exception. When the pungent mix is combined with fiery chilli bean paste, the alchemy is nothing short of sensational. There are many variations to this quintessential Sichuan dish, which can vary immensely when prepared by Hunan or Hubei chefs, some versions being exceedingly hot. Serve on a bed of noodles or rice.

1 Slice the beef into thin strips about 1cm/½in thick, then put them into a bowl. Put the cornflour into a small bowl and blend in the sesame oil and soy sauce. Sprinkle this mixture over the beef and toss to coat. Leave to marinate for 10 minutes.

2 Heat the groundnut oil in a wok and fry the garlic and ginger for 30 seconds, or until light brown. Toss in the beef and stir-fry over a high heat for 1 minute. Add the spring onions, chilli bean paste, five-spice powder, sugar and 45ml/3 tbsp water.

3 Stir the beef and sauce over a high heat for 2 minutes, or until the sauce is thick. Serve immediately, with thick egg noodles or rice, sprinkled with shredded spring onions.

Variation Some variations, especially Cantonese ones, use oyster sauce instead of soy sauce for a more savoury flavour.

Serves 4

450g/1lb sirloin or rump (round) steak
5ml/1 tsp cornflour (cornstarch)
30ml/2 tbsp sesame oil
15ml/1 tbsp dark soy sauce
30ml/2 tbsp groundnut (peanut) oil
2 garlic cloves, crushed
25g/1oz fresh root ginger, chopped
2 spring onions (scallions), cut into
　5cm/2in lengths
15ml/1 tbsp chilli bean paste
　(dou banjiang)
2.5ml/½ tsp five-spice powder
2.5ml/½ tsp caster (superfine) sugar
thick egg noodles or rice, to serve
shredded spring onions, to garnish

Per portion Energy 178kcal/745kJ; Protein 27g;
Carbohydrate 3g, of which sugars 1g; Fat 6g,
of which saturates 2g; Cholesterol 57mg;
Calcium 21mg; Fibre 0.1g; Sodium 153mg

Boiled fiery beef

The Chinese name shui zhu niu rou literally means 'beef boiled in water', so if you encounter this dish in Sichuan, you are apt to think it is a token gesture toward foreigners who are wary of spicy food. However, it is tongue-tinglingly hot from a liberal blend of two of the region's most potent ingredients: Sichuan dried chillies and peppercorns. If these aren't enough to set your palate alight, there is some chilli bean paste here too.

1 Using a sharp knife, slice the beef into thin slices across the grain and put into a shallow dish. Put the cornflour in a small bowl and blend in the wine or sherry, garlic and salt. Sprinkle over the beef and toss to coat evenly. Set aside to marinate while you prepare the sauce.

2 Heat half the oil in a wok over medium-low heat. Add the dried chilli flakes and peppercorns – they should sizzle lightly – and stir for 10 seconds, then pour the oil and spices into a heatproof bowl and leave to cool.

3 Heat the remaining oil in a clean wok and fry the chilli bean paste for about 30 seconds over a medium heat. Add 500ml/17fl oz/generous 2 cups water and the soy sauce, then turn heat to high and bring to the boil.

4 Add the beef and its marinade to the wok, stirring to separate the beef slices. Cook for 2–3 minutes or so, until the beef is just cooked, then transfer the beef and sauce to a serving plate.

5 Heat 15–30ml/2–3 tbsp of the chilli oil mixture, depending on how spicy you want it, in a pan until very hot, then drizzle over the beef – the sauce should sizzle. Serve immediately.

Variation You can cook chicken or pork in the same way.

Serves 4

450g/1lb sirloin or rump (round) steak
5ml/1 tsp cornflour (cornstarch)
30ml/2 tbsp Shaoxing wine or
   dry sherry
2 garlic cloves, crushed
2.5ml/½ tsp salt
100ml/3½fl oz/scant ½ cup
   sunflower oil
8 dried chillies, seeded if you like,
   crushed into coarse flakes
5ml/1 tsp crushed
   Sichuan peppercorns
30ml/2 tbsp chilli bean paste
   (dou banjiang)
15ml/1 tbsp light soy sauce

Cook's tip Make sure your spices are fresh, or the dish will be unpleasantly acrid.

Per portion Energy 399kcal/1653kJ; Protein 27g; Carbohydrate 0g, of which sugars 0g; Fat 16g, of which saturates 5g; Cholesterol 69mg; Calcium 33mg; Fibre 0.3g; Sodium 512mg

Mixed smoked meats

Smoking foods is a particular Sichuan style of cuisine, where the meats absorb the flavour from tea leaves that are used with a variety of other smoking materials. In rural Sichuan, meats will be smoked over bamboo leaves, pine needles, rice straw or even peanut husks and sawdust from aromatic woods, but it is the type of tea that is added that will determine the final flavour. Semi-fermented oolong tea from the Fujian province gives a delicious smokiness, or you can use jasmine tea for a much milder flavour. This is a fairly lengthy recipe, but the results are well worth the effort.

1 Cut each poultry breast and pork steak into two pieces. Put the marinade ingredients into a bowl and mix together, then rub all over meats. Put into a deep dish, cover with clear film (plastic wrap) and chill for at least 8 hours, turning once or twice during this time. Allow to return to room temperature before steaming, and remove the clear film.

2 Transfer the dish to a wok or steamer of simmering water, and steam over a high heat for 15 minutes. Remove the dish and take out the meats. Drain on kitchen paper and set aside.

3 Line a large wok with a double sheet of foil. Mix the smoking materials together and sprinkle them over the base of the wok in an even layer. Put several small Chinese teacups or heatproof eggcups among the smoking material, and put a small wire rack or piece of wire netting on top so that there is a space between the smoking material and the meat.

4 Put the marinated meats on the rack or wire mesh. Turn on the heat to the very lowest setting and cover the wok tightly. Twist and wind several pieces of kitchen paper around the lid so that all the smoke is trapped inside. Smoke for 20 minutes, checking occasionally. Turn off the heat and remove the smoked meats.

5 Heat the vegetable oil in a wok or deep-fryer, then deep-fry the smoked meats, a few pieces at a time. Cook until a crisp skin forms. Cool slightly, then slice thinly. Serve garnished with shredded spring onions, and with some pickled ginger.

Serves 4

225g/8oz duck breast fillet
225g/8oz skinless chicken
   breast fillet
225g/8oz pork rib steak
vegetable oil, for deep-frying
shredded spring onions (scallions),
   to garnish
pickled ginger, to serve

For the marinade
5ml/1 tsp salt
5ml/1 tsp ground
   Sichuan peppercorns
30ml/2 tbsp Shaoxing wine or
   dry sherry
30ml/2 tbsp red fermented tofu
   (tofu ru), finely crumbled

Smoking materials
50g/2oz tea leaves of your choice
3 dried bamboo leaves or 1 lotus
   leaf, roughly chopped
75g/3oz camphor woodchips or
   peanut husks

Per portion Energy 280kcal/1179kJ; Protein 51g; Carbohydrate 2g, of which sugars 0g; Fat 7g, of which saturates 2g; Cholesterol 176mg; Calcium 56mg; Fibre 0g; Sodium 657mg

Rabbit in hot bean sauce

Although game doesn't appear very often on traditional western Chinese menus, when it does, it is cooked with tremendous skill and passion. The bi-annual food and wine event, Food and Hotel Asia (FHA) in Singapore, attracts scores of top chefs from China to display their skills. Here is a wonderful rabbit dish, which was famously prepared there by a Sichuan master. It combines many of the typical vibrant tastes of the region.

1 Cut the rabbit into bitesize pieces, removing as much bone as possible. Bring a large pan of water to the boil and add the onion, Sichuan peppercorns and rabbit pieces. Simmer for 10 minutes, then lift out the rabbit using a slotted spoon. Set aside.

2 Heat the oil in a wok and fry the ginger for 40 seconds until lightly browned. Add the chilli bean paste, soy sauce, hoisin sauce and sesame oil, then stir briefly for 20 seconds.

3 Add the rabbit pieces and stir-fry over a medium heat for 3–4 minutes, or until it is thoroughly covered in the sauce. Garnish each portion with a coriander leaf and a decorative chilli, and serve.

Serves 4

800g/1¾lb rabbit
1 large onion, thinly sliced
5ml/1 tsp Sichuan peppercorns
15m/1 tbsp groundnut (peanut) oil
30ml/2 tbsp grated fresh root ginger
30ml/2 tbsp chilli bean paste
  (dou banjiang)
30ml/2 tbsp light soy sauce
15ml/1 tbsp hoisin sauce
30ml/2 tbsp sesame oil
coriander (cilantro) leaves and
  decorative chillies, to garnish

Variation Use chicken instead of rabbit. You will need a chicken about 1kg/2¼lb in weight or 4 chicken legs.

Per portion Energy 274kcal/1422kJ; Protein 23g; Carbohydrate 8g, of which sugars 5g; Fat 17g, of which saturates 4g; Cholesterol 53mg; Calcium 45mg; Fibre 0.9g; Sodium 676mg

Serves 4

2 pig's kidneys
5ml/1 tsp cornflour (cornstarch)
8 dried Chinese mushrooms,
  soaked for 30 minutes in warm
  water until soft
15ml/1 tbsp groundnut (peanut) oil
3 fresh green chillies, seeded
  and sliced
5ml/1 tsp chilli paste
15ml/1 tbsp light soy sauce
30ml/2 tbsp rice wine or vinegar
15ml/1 tbsp sesame oil
1 green (bell) pepper, cut into chunks
75g/3oz bamboo shoot slices
fresh coriander (cilantro) leaves,
  to garnish

Per portion Energy 186kcal/776kJ; Protein 14g;
Carbohydrate 9g, of which sugars 2g; Fat 11g,
of which saturates 2g; Cholesterol 333mg;
Calcium 23mg; Fibre 1g; Sodium 451mg

Hot-and-sour kidneys

In Chinese cooking, particularly in Chengdu, Sichuan's capital city, offal (organ meats) is much revered for its robust flavour and nutritional value. Kidneys have an especially strong flavour, and when cooked with rich sauces they are transformed into culinary masterpieces. The kidneys in this recipe are cooked in a hot-and-sour blend of flavourings, which is typical of much regional cooking in western China.

1 Cut the kidneys horizontally to make two flat halves. With a sharp knife, trim off the white membrane. Soak the kidneys in cold water for 15 minutes, then drain on kitchen paper. Put the cornflour in a bowl and gradually blend with 75ml/5 tbsp water. Set aside.

2 Make criss-cross cuts halfway down the outer side of each kidney half, but do not cut all the way through. Cut each half into three or four pieces. Quarter the softened mushrooms.

3 Heat the oil in a wok and fry the green chillies for 30 seconds, then add the chilli paste, soy sauce, wine or vinegar and sesame oil. Stir-fry for 1 minute, then add the mushrooms, green pepper and bamboo shoots. Stir for 1 minute and add the kidney pieces.

4 Stir over a high heat for 30 seconds, then add the cornflour mixture. Cook for 1 minute more, or until the sauce is thick and the kidneys are cooked through – they will shrink a little when done. Serve hot, garnished with coriander.

Rice and noodles

"Have you eaten rice?" is a greeting used throughout China, which takes for granted that 'rice' is another word for 'food'. It is really a rhetorical question that addresses one's wellbeing, the grain being fundamental to life itself. This staple food, which is grown throughout the country (apart from the far north), forms the single most important element of almost every meal, though people from western China are also reliant on a range of steamed breads, and an impressive variety of noodles.

Speedy stir-fries and sticky parcels

In western China, the majority of rice is grown in Yunnan, Guizhou and Sichuan provinces. When reference is made to 'sticky rice' it can refer to any type of rice that is high in starchy molecules, which form a gel enclosing the water within their strands.

Throughout China, when rice is cooked, there are two basic methods – boiling or steaming. Once rice is cooked, it can be used as the basis for the iconic fried rice. Starchier rice such as glutinous is best soaked for several hours and then steamed or boiled. Sichuan, Hubei and Hunan chefs use this to encase savoury or sweet fillings and then wrap the whole thing in lotus or bamboo leaves to create tempting parcels.

While rice is the fundamental staple in some Chinese regions, in the western provinces, noodles and other wheat flour products are equally popular carbohydrates. They are eaten at all hours of the day in Sichuan and Hunan, whether simply stir-fried with some vegetables or enriched with meat and fish for a more nourishing dish.

Noodles take on an extraordinary variety of shapes, some as wide as lasagne and others so thin they resemble silk thread. The range is endless: fresh or dried, round or flat, and made from wheat, mung beans or, less often, rice flour. In Chengdu, hand-made noodles are expertly made on the streets and in restaurants: noodle-makers can be seen kneading large lumps of dough, pulling and stretching every which way until, miraculously, they are transformed into fine or thick threads.

Serves 4

150g/5oz/generous ²/₃ cup black
  glutinous rice, soaked overnight
90g/3½oz smoked ham, diced into
  1cm/½in cubes
90g/3½oz skinless chicken breast,
  diced into 1cm/½in cubes
30ml/2 tbsp light soy sauce
15ml/1 tbsp sesame oil
salt and ground white pepper
coriander (cilantro) leaves or chopped
  spring onions (scallions), to garnish

Black rice porridge

Grown throughout subtropical China, black rice is particularly common in Sichuan and Hunan. It is generally glutinous and has to be treated like normal glutinous rice, needing a long soak to soften the dense grains.

1 Drain the rice and place in a large pan with 2 litres/3½ pints/9 cups water. Bring to the boil, then reduce the heat to low and simmer for 45 minutes. Check occasionally that it doesn't become too thick, adding more hot water if necessary. The consistency should be like a creamy porridge.

2 Add the smoked ham and chicken to the rice and cook for a further 5 minutes, then add the soy sauce, sesame oil, and the salt and pepper. Continue to simmer for 10 minutes more, then serve, garnished with coriander leaves or chopped spring onions.

Cook's tips
• All glutinous rice absorbs lots of water, so it is best to soak it overnight to get a creamy porridge when cooked.
• Century eggs make a tasty addition to the dish. These are duck's eggs that have been pickled until they their whites turn a gelatinous black and the yolks a matt grey. They can be cut up and added to the porridge for the last few minutes of cooking, when they will impart a distinctive flavour. Century eggs do not need to be cooked and can be eaten as they are.

Per portion Energy 246kcal/10267kJ; Protein 15g;
Carbohydrate 29g, of which sugars 1g; Fat 7g,
of which saturates 2g; Cholesterol 16mg;
Calcium 10mg; Fibre 0.2g; Sodium 1097mg

Pineapple rice

This recipe of rice with pineapple and ham comes from Yunnan, which has a rugged terrain dissected by deep valleys and crossed by mountains. It has a subtropical, humid climate where rice, tea, peanuts, pineapples and other tropical fruits grow in abundance. The province is home to the Dai people, hill tribes who are linguistically part of the Thai family, so it not surprising that pineapple, a typical staple of Thai cuisine, features in dishes of the region. Yunnan is also famed for its dry-cured ham from the Xuanwei region, which is rare outside China. Prosciutto or Serrano ham make good substitutes.

1 Heat the oil in a wok and fry the garlic for 30 seconds. Push it to one side and pour in the eggs. Cook until set, then cut up roughly with a wok ladle. Add the cold rice and stir for 2 minutes over a medium heat.

2 Add the pineapple, ham, spring onions, peas, pepper and sesame oil, then continue to stir-fry rapidly over a medium heat for 5 minutes. Serve hot, garnished with an extra sprinkling of ground Sichuan peppercorns, if you like.

Cook's tip The best rice for frying is cold, cooked rice, whether you use long grain or jasmine. If you have kept it overnight, rake it with a fork to loosen the grains before frying. The important thing to remember when you are cooking the rice is that you must use a little less water than normal so you get firmer grains that are less likely to clump together.

Variation This dish is ideal for using up leftover meat, chicken or seafood.

Serves 4

30ml/2 tbsp groundnut (peanut) oil
3 garlic cloves, crushed
2 eggs, lightly beaten
200g/7oz/1 cup long grain or jasmine
    rice, cooked and left to become
    cold, or 400g/14oz/2 cups cold
    cooked rice
150g/5oz fresh pineapple, finely diced
75g/3oz dry-cured ham, diced into
    5mm/¼in cubes
2 spring onions (scallions), chopped
25g/1oz/2 tbsp garden peas
2.5ml/½ tsp ground Sichuan
    peppercorns, plus extra to garnish
15ml/1 tbsp sesame oil

Per portion Energy 403kcal/1692kJ; Protein 13g; Carbohydrate 48g, of which sugars 4g; Fat 19g, of which saturates 4g; Cholesterol 116mg; Calcium 61mg; Fibre 1.1g; Sodium 422mg

Glutinous rice in bamboo leaves

Blade-shaped bamboo leaves make versatile wrappers and also impart a pleasant flavour to whatever food you wrap in them. Although they are usually used to wrap individual dumplings – traditionally for the dumpling festival in China – they can be overlapped in a container to wrap a larger amount, such as the rice and stuffing in this recipe. When the leaves are opened at the table, the lovely aromas are released.

1 Soak the glutinous rice in water for at least 6 hours or overnight. Drain well. Spread the rice in a steamer tray over simmering water. Steam over a high heat for 20 minutes – do not add salt. Fluff up the rice using a fork and then stir in the salt. Set aside.

2 To make the stuffing, drain the shiitake mushrooms and rinse well to remove any grit. Cut off and discard the stalks and cut the caps into small dice.

3 Heat the oil in a wok over a high heat. Fry the garlic for 30 seconds, then add the pork and mushrooms, and stir-fry for 5 minutes. Add the remaining ingredients with 100ml/ 3½fl oz/scant ½ cup water. Partially cover and cook for 5 minutes, stirring occasionally. Cover and set aside.

4 Plunge the bamboo leaves in a pan of simmering water for 1–2 minutes, to blanch them until softened and flexible. Place 3 or 4 leaves in a deep dish or casserole, fanning them out to cover the base and sides. Spread half the rice on top of leaves, then top with the pork mixture. Cover with the remaining rice and pat into a neat mound. Cover with the rest of the bamboo leaves, and tuck in the edges to seal. Put the dish into a steamer over simmering water.

5 Steam the parcel over a high heat for 20–25 minutes, or until fully heated through. Serve, with a hoisin or black vinegar dip.

Variation Shelled roasted or boiled chestnuts, left whole or chopped, make a great addition to the filling.

Serves 4

400g/14oz glutinous rice
5ml/1 tsp salt
6–8 dried bamboo leaves
hoisin or Xinkiang black vinegar,
  to serve

For the stuffing
4 dried shiitake mushrooms, soaked
  in hot water for 30 minutes
30ml/2 tbsp groundnut (peanut) oil
2 garlic cloves, crushed
200g/7oz lean pork, diced
30ml/2 tbsp light soy sauce
30ml/2 tbsp oyster sauce
15ml/1 tbsp sesame oil
5ml/1 tsp ground black pepper
1 small spring onion
  (scallion), chopped

Per portion Energy 548kcal/2288kJ; Protein 20g;
Carbohydrate 80g, of which sugars 1g; Fat 15g,
of which saturates 3g; Cholesterol 32mg;
Calcium 29mg; Fibre 0.5g; Sodium 1377mg

Clay-pot rice with Chinese salt fish

This Sichuan dish is real comfort food all over China, especially among rural folk. Cooked first in an ordinary pan and than served in a heated clay pot, it's like a casserole and is full of flavour. Seasonings vary from region to region, as do the meats and seafood. Look for salt fish made from meaty fish such as haddock or cod. If these are not available, Portuguese dried salt fish, bacalao, can be used but it requires soaking first.

1 Heat the oil in a wok and fry the salt fish over a medium heat until fragrant and crisp. Remove the fish from the pan and leave to cool. Fry the sliced sausage for 2 minutes over a low heat and remove.

2 Put the rice in a pan and add water to come up to 2.5cm/1in above the level of the rice. Bring to the boil and simmer, covered, for 20–25 minutes, or until tender.

3 While the rice is cooking, heat the oil remaining in the pan, add the garlic and fry for 30 seconds. Add the chicken, mushrooms, oyster sauce, sesame oil, ground black pepper and soy sauce, then stir-fry for 2 minutes. Add 75ml/5 tbsp water and stir for 2 minutes, or until thick.

4 Heap the chicken mixture on to the rice for the last five minutes of cooking and blend well. If you like, heat a clay pot in a hot oven for 10 minutes and transfer the rice to it for serving, although you can, of course, just serve from the pan.

Serves 4

45ml/3 tbsp vegetable oil
90g/3½oz Chinese salt fish, cut into small dice
1 Chinese sausage, thinly sliced
400g/14oz/2 cups jasmine rice
2 garlic cloves, crushed
200g/7oz skinless chicken breast fillet, diced
4 dried Chinese mushrooms, soaked and chopped
30ml/2 tbsp oyster sauce
30ml/2 tbsp sesame oil
5ml/1 tsp ground black pepper
15ml/1 tbsp light soy sauce

Per portion Energy 706kcal/2927kJ; Protein 30g; Carbohydrate 92g, of which sugars 0g; Fat 27g, of which saturates 3g; Cholesterol 35mg; Calcium 80mg; Fibre 0.5g; Sodium 1968mg

Dan dan noodles

Of all the Sichuan street foods, this dish has probably the highest profile and is also the most well-travelled. It was originally sold by itinerant hawkers in Chengdu, and the name is believed to derive from the bamboo pole, or dan, slung across the hawkers' shoulders. The dan held baskets at each end containing cooking paraphernalia such as a small stove and other kitchen equipment. The hawkers announced their arrival by shouting 'Dan dan mien!'

1 Heat the oil in a wok and fry the pickled vegetables briefly for 30 seconds. Remove from the pan and put in a bowl. Set aside.

2 To make the topping, heat the oil in a wok over a high heat and stir-fry the pork or beef for 1 minute.

3 Add the wine or sherry, soy sauce and yellow bean paste. Stir-fry for 1 minute more, or until the meat is cooked through.

4 Add the spring onions to the pickled vegetables in the bowl and stir in the soy sauce, chilli paste or oil, vinegar and peppercorns.

5 Plunge the noodles into a pan of rapidly boiling water and cook them for 1–2 minutes, or until they are just tender but not limp. Drain the noodles thoroughly and transfer them to a serving bowl.

6 Toss the seasoned vegetables into the noodles, then top with the meat mixture. Mix well before serving.

Cook's tip There are several types of fresh wheat noodles available today, but for this recipe use one that is the thickness of spaghetti or even spaghettini.

Serves 4

15ml/1 tbsp groundnut (peanut) oil
45g/1¾oz/3 tbsp Sichuan pickled vegetables, chopped
4 spring onions (scallions), chopped
30ml/2 tbsp light soy sauce
30ml/2 tbsp fresh chilli paste or chilli oil
15ml/1 tbsp Xinkiang black vinegar
5ml/1 tsp Sichuan peppercorns, finely ground
350g/12oz thin fresh wheat noodles (see Cook's Tip)

For the topping
15ml/1 tbsp groundnut (peanut) oil
115g/4oz/½ cup minced (ground) pork or beef, not too lean
15ml/1 tbsp Chinese wine or dry sherry
15ml/1 tbsp dark soy sauce
10ml/2 tsp yellow bean paste

Per portion Energy 531kcal/2231kJ; Protein 17g; Carbohydrate 70g, of which sugars 4g; Fat 22g, of which saturates 3g; Cholesterol 18mg; Calcium 46mg; Fibre 2.9g; Sodium 815mg

Cold noodles

Although cold noodles are really a preserve of the Japanese, Chinese chefs also make the occasional cool dish during the hot and humid summer months. This recipe is believed to have originated in Shanghai but found its way to north-western China over time. It makes a refreshing change when the summer temperatures soar and hot, extremely spicy food no longer seems appealing.

1 Soak the dried prawns in warm water for 10 minutes. Drain, then remove any pieces of dried shell. Wash and drain again. Chop the prawns up roughly, then put them into a serving bowl. Add the soy sauce and rice wine or vinegar, and stir to coat.

2 Plunge the noodles into a bowl of boiling water, or according to the packet instructions, until softened. Drain in a colander, then transfer to a serving bowl. Drizzle a little sesame oil all over to prevent the strands sticking together, then set aside to cool completely.

3 Stir the sesame oil and spring onions into the dried prawn mixture. Peel the cucumber and cut out the soft core, then cut into fine shreds. Put on to a small plate or serving bowl.

4 To serve, toss the prawn mixture and cucumber shreds with the noodles at the table, and serve with side dishes of rice wine or vinegar (with dried chilli flakes, if you like) and pickled vegetables, so that diners can season their noodles with their own choice of flavours.

Serves 4

25g/1oz/2 tbsp dried prawns (shrimp)
30ml/2 tbsp light soy sauce,
  plus extra to serve
30ml/2 tbsp rice wine or vinegar
450g/1lb fresh wheat or egg noodles,
  the thickness of spaghetti
15ml/1 tbsp sesame oil, plus extra
  for drizzling
2 spring onions (scallions), chopped
½ cucumber
25g/1oz/2 tbsp Sichuan pickled
  vegetables, soaked and chopped,
  to serve
rice wine or vinegar and dried chilli
  flakes (optional), to serve

Cook's tip If you want a spicy version, add 1 tbsp chilli paste to the dried prawn mixture.

Per portion Energy 501kcal/2118kJ; Protein 18g; Carbohydrate 88g, of which sugars 4g; Fat 11g, of which saturates 1g; Cholesterol 0mg; Calcium 60mg; Fibre 3.6; Sodium 622mg

Serves 2

150g/5oz mung bean noodles

200g/7oz/scant 1 cup minced
  (ground) pork

30ml/2 tbsp dark soy sauce

5ml/1 tsp caster (superfine) sugar

10ml/2 tsp cornflour (cornstarch)

5ml/1 tsp chilli paste

2.5ml/½ tsp ground black pepper

45ml/3 tbsp vegetable oil

2 garlic cloves, finely chopped

2 spring onions (scallions),
  finely chopped

1 red chilli, seeded and finely
  chopped, to garnish

Cook's tip Mung bean noodles do
not become mushy even when
cooked for a long time. Thai or Korean
brands have even better resilience.

Per portion Energy 658kcal/2743kJ; Protein 26g;
Carbohydrate 71g, of which sugars 5g; Fat 29g,
of which saturates 4g; Cholesterol 63mg;
Calcium 37mg; Fibre 0.3g; Sodium 1152mg

Minced pork with glass noodles

*This favourite Chongqing dish of mung bean noodles (translucent vermicelli)
and minced pork is fondly known as 'ants climbing trees', so called because
the cooked mince looks rather like ants clambering over a silky mound.
Flavoured with garlic, chilli and soy, it is a truly delicious combination.*

1 Soak the noodles in warm water for 20 minutes, or until they swell to almost double their
dry size. The strands should be slightly gelatinous and slippery. Drain and set aside.

2 Put the minced pork in a large bowl and add the soy sauce, sugar, cornflour, chilli paste
and pepper. Mix well together.

3 Heat the oil and fry the garlic until light brown, then add the onions. Fry for 1 minute.
Add the minced pork mixture, stirring vigorously with a spoon to break it up.

4 Stir-fry for 2–3 minutes, or until the pork is well cooked through. Add 120ml/4fl oz/½ cup
water and the soaked noodles.

5 Toss for 20–30 seconds, or until the noodles are just tender and have absorbed the sauce.
Serve, garnished with the chopped red chilli.

Serves 4

250g/9oz fresh wheat noodles
115g/4oz lean pork, fat removed
30ml/2 tbsp groundnut (peanut) oil
2 garlic cloves, chopped
30ml/2 tbsp oyster sauce
2.5ml/½ tsp ground black pepper
65g/2½oz beansprouts

Stir-fried noodles with pork

One of the most basic noodle dishes, this Shaanxi staple is perfect comfort food when you are pushed for time. You could even use instant noodles; there are dozens available, many with sachets of flavourings enclosed. Use these or prepare your own – fresh wheat noodles need only to be briefly blanched. Beansprouts are the perfect crunchy complement to the soft noodles, to give the dish its yin and yang balance.

1 Plunge the noodles into a pan of boiling water for 1 minute, to blanch briefly, then drain. Slice the pork into thin strips.

2 Heat the oil in a wok and fry the garlic for 30 seconds, then add the pork strips, oyster sauce and pepper. Stir-fry for 2 minutes, or until the pork is cooked through.

3 Add the beansprouts and noodles, then stir-fry for 2 minutes over a high heat. Add 90ml/ 6 tbsp water. Stir to blend well and serve hot.

Cook's tip For vegetarians, substitute pork with the equivalent amount of half and half sliced mushrooms or whole button (white) mushrooms and dried tofu.

Per portion Energy 358kcal/1506kJ; Protein 14g; Carbohydrate 50g, of which sugars 2g; Fat 13g, of which saturates 2g; Cholesterol 18mg; Calcium 23mg; Fibre 2.1g; Sodium 334mg

Beef and chive noodles

Sichuan noodle dishes have a reputation for being hearty, as they are meant to be complete meals in themselves. On busy days, families will fry up a batch and everyone helps themselves. Accompaniments such as fried shallots, sliced chillies and chopped spring onions or leeks are often added at the table. This dish uses Chinese chives, which are a favourite in Sichuan for their delicious crunch, and is accompanied by some simple piquant flavourings.

1 First, make the serving accompaniments. Put the green chillies into a small dish and mix in the dark soy sauce. Put the shredded ginger into a small dish and add the black vinegar. Put the chopped coriander into a small dish.

2 Cook the noodles in a pan of boiling water for 5 minutes or according to the packet instructions. Drain and set aside, raking them with chopsticks or a fork to separate the strands.

3 Slice the beef into thin strips and put into a bowl. Put the sesame oil into a small bowl and blend in the peppercorns, soy sauce and cornflour. Pour over the beef and toss to coat completely. Leave to marinate for 10 minutes.

4 Heat the oil in a wok and fry the garlic and ginger for 30 seconds. Add the beef and its marinade and stir-fry for 2 minutes.

5 Add the noodles and chives, then cook, stirring, for 1 minute. Add 120ml/4fl oz/½ cup water and stir until the sauce is thick. Serve with the accompaniments.

Serves 4

300g/11oz dry egg noodles
200g/7oz beef sirloin
30ml/2 tbsp sesame oil
5ml/1 tsp ground Sichuan peppercorns
30ml/2 tbsp dark soy sauce
5ml/1 tsp cornflour (cornstarch)
30ml/2 tbsp groundnut (peanut) oil
4 garlic cloves, chopped
25g/1oz fresh root ginger, shredded
75g/3oz Chinese chives, cut into
　5cm/2in lengths

To serve
2 fresh green chillies, seeded
　and chopped
30ml/2 tbsp dark soy sauce
15ml/1 tbsp grated ginger
30ml/2 tbsp Xinkiang black vinegar
chopped fresh coriander (cilantro)

Per portion Energy 374kcal/1582kJ; Protein 22g; Carbohydrate 56g, of which sugars 3g; Fat 9g, of which saturates 3g; Cholesterol 48mg; Calcium 44mg; Fibre 2.7g; Sodium 706mg

Vegetables

Although the best-known dishes outside of China are highly dependent on meat, poultry and seafood, in virtually every Chinese meal, whether grand or humble, vegetables are important ingredients. Markets in Sichuan, Hunan, Hubei and Yunnan are literally overflowing with an astonishing array of green produce, and in rural areas, vegetables are hugely important as meat and poultry can be expensive and hard to find. There are relatively few committed vegetarians in the country but, as a rule, vegetarian cooking in western China tends to be simple and flavourful, making the most of fresh ingredients and pungent aromatics.

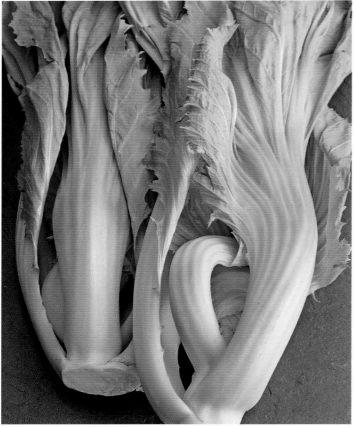

Crisp and fresh, pickled and fried

The vegetables in western China tend to be pickled or stir-fried in a multitude of dishes. Various types of aubergines (eggplants), ranging from white to deep purple, slender to plump, and tiny to large, are available all year round. They are deep-fried, then stir-fried with a medley of flavoursome ingredients in the classic dish Shredded Aubergine.

Crunchy beansprouts pop up everywhere, eaten raw or stir-fried. Bamboo shoots are prolific here because of the sub-tropical climate, and have a chameleon-like quality, absorbing other flavours while imparting their own distinctive scent.

Chives are found in three forms throughout China: green chives (jiu cai) with flat slim-bladed leaves; yellow chives (jiu huang), which are grown under a cloche or in the dark; and flowering chives (also known as garlic chives) with sturdy round stems tipped with pointed green buds. All feature prominently in Sichuan and Hubei cooking and are much loved for their garlicky flavour.

Mustard greens are often pickled to be used as a robust foil for other ingredients. Most versatile, they turn up in many a vegetarian soup, as a salting agent or as a stir-fried vegetable in their own right. Fresh coriander (cilantro) and celery are used imaginatively, not merely as garnishes but as featured players in bold salads.

It is, however, the Sichuan bean, similar to the green bean, that has become truly representative of classic Sichuan vegetarian cooking.

Pickled mustard greens

Mustard greens, called qing cai in Mandarin or gai choy in Cantonese, are most often sun-dried, rubbed with salt, and pickled in spices and sugar in Guizhou. These large, fleshy-stalked vegetables with bright green leaves have a crisp and slightly bitter edge when stir-fried, but when pickled they have a robust flavour and texture. In China the pickled greens are left to mature for months in earthenware or ceramic crocks – they are then known as ya cai in Mandarin. Sometimes, only the tender leaves are pickled, and you can distinguish these from the pickled stalks, as the leaves are a dark jade green and floppy.

1 Put 550ml/18fl oz/2½ cups water in a pan and bring to the boil. Add the salt and stir to dissolve. Remove from the heat and leave to cool completely.

2 Prepare a large pickling jar or a non-metal bowl by pouring in boiling water to sterilize it, then drain thoroughly. Pour the cold brine into the jar or bowl.

3 Remove the stalks from the chillies, but leave them whole. Add to the brine with the Sichuan peppercorns, rice wine or vinegar, sugar and ginger, and stir well.

4 Cut the mustard greens into pieces, each about 5cm/2in, then wash and pat dry thoroughly. If possible, dry them in the sun for a few hours.

5 Put the mustard greens in the jar or bowl and put a clean plate on top. Weight down with a heavy object such as a stone pestle, to make sure the vegetables are completely immersed. Cover tightly with clear film (plastic wrap) or a large plate and store in a cool, dark place for at least four days. The pickled greens are best after a week.

6 When you want to serve the pickled greens, drain them, squeeze out any excess liquid and cut them into shreds. Top with a little sugar and fresh red chillies.

Serves 6–8

45ml/3 tbsp crushed rock or sea salt
5 fresh red chillies
2.5ml/½ tsp ground
  Sichuan peppercorns
15ml/1 tbsp rice wine or vinegar
15ml/1 tbsp soft light brown sugar
25g/1oz fresh root ginger, grated
450g/1lb mustard greens
1 litre/1¾ pints/4 cups water
sugar and fresh red chillies, to serve

Cook's tip This is a versatile pickle that can be added to pork and chicken stir-fries, and to omelettes.

Per portion Energy 26kcal/111kJ; Protein 2g; Carbohydrate 5g, of which sugars 3g; Fat 0g, of which saturates 0g; Cholesterol 0mg; Calcium 84mg; Fibre 1.9g; Sodium 1467mg

Pickled celery and coriander salad

Serves 4

300g/11oz Chinese or English
  celery sticks
10ml/2 tsp salt
75g/3oz fresh coriander (cilantro)
5ml/1 tsp ground
  Sichuan peppercorns
5ml/1 tsp caster (superfine) sugar
30ml/2 tbsp rice wine or vinegar
25ml/1½ tbsp sesame oil
25g/1oz/2 tbsp roasted peanuts,
  coarsely chopped
15ml/1 tbsp sesame seeds,
  lightly toasted

Fresh coriander might not be an obvious salad ingredient but its flavour goes marvellously with celery in this delicious dish from Hubei. It is the simplest of salads, sharp with vinegar and aromatic with ground Sichuan peppercorns, which have a distinctive liquorice flavour. Western celery sticks have only the barest frill of leaves, whereas Chinese or Thai celery have long stalks, more leaves and a more pronounced flavour. Use whichever is available.

1 Slice the celery thickly into 1cm/½in wide pieces on the diagonal. (You can include the leaves, if you wish.)

2 Put the celery in a colander and sprinkle with the salt. Leave for 25 minutes.

3 Remove the thickest, toughest stalks from the coriander and chop the remainder roughly.

4 Put the ground Sichuan peppercorns into a bowl and add the sugar, rice wine or vinegar and sesame oil. Whisk well to blend and dissolve the sugar.

5 Squeeze out as much moisture as you can from the celery and pat dry with kitchen paper. (If you prefer your celery less salty, briefly rinse under running water first.)

6 Place the celery in a bowl, add the coriander and the peppercorn dressing, and toss well. Transfer to a serving plate and top with chopped peanuts and sesame seeds, then serve.

Variation Although the peppercorns provide the requisite spice, adding a chopped fresh red chilli will give the salad a fiery lift, if you like your food hot.

Per portion Energy 98kcal/405kJ; Protein 2g; Carbohydrate 3g, of which sugars 2g; Fat 9g, of which saturates 1g; Cholesterol 0mg; Calcium 73mg; Fibre 1.2g; Sodium 1044mg

Spicy cucumber salad

Another Hubei staple, this fresh-tasting pickle is flavoured with mustard, chillies and ginger, though there are many taste variations on the theme throughout the region. Leave the flavours to blend for an hour before serving, but then eat the salad while it is fresh, with grilled meats and chicken. It should be eaten on the day it is made, as the cucumber will become mushy if it is left too long.

1 Quarter the cucumber lengthways and cut out the soft core. Slice each strip into 1cm/½in thick pieces on the diagonal. Sprinkle with salt and leave for 30 minutes.

2 Pound the garlic and ginger to a fine paste using a mortar and pestle. Transfer to a bowl and add the brown sugar, rice wine or vinegar and mustard. Stir well.

3 Squeeze out the moisture from the cucumber pieces and pat dry. Put into a serving bowl. Cut the chillies into thin strips and add to the cucumber. Add the garlic and ginger dressing and mix well. Cover and leave for 1 hour. Serve, sprinkled with sesame seeds.

Variation If you like, you can make this recipe using half cucumber and half mooli (daikon), salted, squeezed and drained as for the cucumber.

Serves 4

1 whole cucumber
5ml/1 tsp salt
4 garlic cloves, peeled and chopped
3 thick slices fresh root ginger,
  peeled and chopped
5ml/1 tsp soft light brown sugar
30ml/2 tbsp rice wine or vinegar
5ml/1 tsp prepared English or
  Dijon mustard
4 fresh red chillies, seeded
15ml/1 tbsp sesame seeds

Per portion Energy 42kcal/174kJ; Protein 2g; Carbohydrate 4g, of which sugars 3g; Fat 2g, of which saturates 0g; Cholesterol 0mg; Calcium 40mg; Fibre 0.9g; Sodium 555mg

Spicy green beans

This dish has spawned many a regional version purporting to be 'Sichuan-style', but few come close to the original, which uses a special bean grown in the province, called the 'four-season bean'. However, green beans come close. Sichuan preserved vegetables are another authentic ingredient, which are bought as a dry product, pickled in salt, that has to be soaked and rinsed before use.

1 Soak the dried prawns for 15 minutes, or until soft. Cut the beans in half, if they are more than 7.5cm/3in long. Finely chop the soaked dried prawns and preserved vegetables.

2 Heat the vegetable oil in a wok over a medium heat or in a deep-fryer. Plunge the beans into the oil for 1–2 minutes, or until lightly blistered. Lift out and drain well on kitchen paper.

3 In a clean wok, heat the groundnut oil over a high heat and fry the spring onions and ginger for 30 seconds.

4 Add the dried shrimps and preserved vegetables and stir-fry for 1 minute. Add the salt, sugar, chilli bean paste, sesame oil, fried beans and rice wine or vinegar. Stir rapidly over a high heat for 30 seconds, then add 30ml/2 tbsp water. Stir for 1 minute more, or until the beans are just tender, and serve hot.

Cook's tip You can use 15ml/1 tbsp chopped dried or fresh red chillies instead of the chilli bean paste, if you like, though you won't get the characteristic Sichuan flavour that you would get with the chilli bean paste.

Serves 4

15g/¹⁄₂ oz/1 tbsp dried
  prawns (shrimp)
450g/1lb green beans, trimmed
25g/1oz/2 tbsp Sichuan preserved
  vegetables, soaked for 15 minutes
  and drained
vegetable oil, for deep-frying
30ml/2 tbsp groundnut (peanut) oil
2 spring onions (scallions), chopped
25g/1oz fresh root ginger, grated
pinch of salt
2.5ml/¹⁄₂ tsp caster (superfine) sugar
30ml/2 tbsp chilli bean paste
  (dou banjiang)
10ml/2 tsp sesame oil
5ml/1 tsp rice wine or vinegar

Per portion Energy 292kcal/1204kJ; Protein 5g; Carbohydrate 5g, of which sugars 3g; Fat 28g, of which saturates 4g; Cholesterol 0mg; Calcium 53mg; Fibre 2.5g; Sodium 183mg

Mixed mushroom stir-fry

Yunnan chefs are adept at cooking the many varieties of mushrooms found in the region, the most popular being dried mushrooms, straw mushrooms and oyster mushrooms. Chinese dried mushrooms are available in different grades; the premium ones are those that have large fissures on their caps. These symbolize prosperity and good luck, and are called hua ku (floral mushrooms) in Mandarin. You can use any mixture, or even just one type.

1 Drain and rinse the canned mushrooms. Cut off the hard stalks from the soaked dried mushrooms. Cut all the mushrooms into similar-sized pieces.

2 Heat the oil in a wok and fry the ginger and garlic for 30 seconds, or until golden brown, then add the mushrooms. Stir-fry for 2 minutes. Put the cornflour into a bowl and blend in 60ml/4 tbsp water. Add the oyster sauce to the wok with the soy sauce, pepper and cornflour mixture.

3 Stir until the sauce is thick and serve hot, garnished with coriander leaves.

Cook's tip
If you are using dried mushrooms, do not discard the water for soaking. Strain through a fine sieve (strainer) and use 60ml/4 tbsp instead of the water for blending with the cornflour.

Serves 4

200g/7oz canned straw mushrooms, drained and rinsed
200g/7oz dried Chinese mushrooms, soaked for 30 minutes in warm water until soft
200g/7oz canned button (white) or oyster mushrooms
30ml/2 tbsp groundnut (peanut) oil
2 slices fresh root ginger, chopped
3 garlic cloves, chopped
5ml/1 tsp cornflour (cornstarch)
30ml/2 tbsp oyster sauce
15ml/1 tbsp soy sauce
2.5ml/½ tsp ground black pepper
coriander (cilantro) leaves, to garnish

Per portion Energy 238kcal/993kJ; Protein 8g; Carbohydrate 34g, of which sugars 1g; Fat 9g, of which saturates 2g; Cholesterol 0mg; Calcium 50mg; Fibre 0.6g; Sodium 731mg

Serves 4

450g/1lb cooked bamboo shoots,
 thinly sliced
2 garlic cloves, crushed
30ml/2 tbsp groundnut (peanut) oil
30ml/2 tbsp oyster sauce
30ml/2 tbsp sesame oil
15ml/1 tbsp yellow bean sauce
5ml/1 tsp caster (superfine) sugar
5ml/1 tsp cornflour (cornstarch)
coriander (cilantro) leaves, to garnish

Variation Add other vegetables,
such as courgettes (zucchini), mooli
(daikon) and carrots. Cut them into
similar sizes to the bamboo shoots
so that they cook at the same time.

Per portion Energy 168kcal/693kJ; Protein 2g;
Carbohydrate 6g, of which sugars 3g; Fat 15g,
of which saturates 3g; Cholesterol 0mg;
Calcium 21mg; Fibre 2g; Sodium 317mg

Stir-fried bamboo shoots

*Bamboo shoots are cooked throughout China and are much loved for their
taste and firm texture that never goes mushy. This recipe uses the bold
flavours of oyster sauce and yellow bean sauce to give the bamboo shoots
a real richness. They are sold in many forms: fresh, canned cooked,
vacuum-packed cooked, fermented, pickled with chillies, slim young
shoots packed in water, and so on, and are widely available.*

1 If using canned bamboo shoots, soak them in fresh water for 1 hour. Drain well and pat
lightly dry with kitchen paper.

2 Heat the oil in a wok over a high heat. Fry the garlic for 45 seconds, then add the bamboo
shoots. Stir-fry vigorously for 1 minute, then add the oyster sauce, sesame oil, yellow bean
sauce and sugar.

3 Fry for 1 minute more, then add 105ml/7 tbsp water. Simmer for 2–3 minutes, or until the
sauce is reduced. Blend the cornflour with 15ml/1 tbsp water, then add this to the wok and
cook until the sauce is thickened and glossy. Serve hot, garnished with coriander.

Serves 4

200g/7oz firm tofu
30ml/2 tbsp groundnut (peanut) oil
450g/1lb Chinese chives, cut into
  5cm/2in lengths
30ml/2 tbsp light soy sauce
2.5ml/½ tsp ground black pepper
15ml/1 tbsp sesame oil

Stir-fried chive stems

Garlic stems, also called Chinese chives or garlic chives, are quite different from common chives, being thicker and juicier, rather like green beans, and tipped with small pale-green heads. They have a pronounced green-onion and garlic flavour, so when they are used in a recipe like this one, there is no need to add garlic, which is otherwise standard in most stir-fried vegetable dishes.

1 Cut the tofu into four squares and again into thin slices, each about 5mm/¼in thick.

2 Heat the oil in a wok over a high heat. Add the tofu and fry for 1 minute, or until lightly browned on both sides. Do not over-stir or you will break up the pieces.

3 Push the tofu to one side, add the chives and stir-fry for 1 minute, taking care not to break up the tofu. Add the soy sauce, pepper, sesame oil and 60ml/4 tbsp water, and stir for 1 minute more, or until the water has evaporated and the chives are just tender. Serve hot.

Per portion Energy 167kcal/690kJ; Protein 7g;
Carbohydrate 3g, of which sugars 3g; Fat 14g,
of which saturates 2g; Cholesterol 0mg;
Calcium 353mg; Fibre 2.1g; Sodium 542mg

Stir-fried spicy courgettes

Courgettes can be stir-fried if you use the young, firm ones. Do not peel them, as most of the nutrients are just under the skin, which is not fibrous. With older courgettes, however, it is best to remove the skin.

1 Slice the courgettes into thick strips, about 2cm x 7.5cm/³⁄₄in x 3in. Bring a small pan of water to the boil and plunge in the courgettes. Cook for 1 minute to blanch them. Drain.

2 Heat the oil in a wok and fry the ginger and garlic for 1 minute, then add the blanched courgettes. Stir-fry over a high heat for 1 minute, then add the peppercorns, soy sauce, sugar and oyster sauce.

3 Cook, stirring, for 1 more minute, then add 30ml/2 tbsp water. Bring to a quick boil and serve hot.

Variation For a change, smaller courgettes can be cut into thin rings and fried in the same way.

Serves 4

450g/1lb courgettes (zucchini)
30ml/2 tbsp groundnut (peanut) oil
25g/1oz fresh root ginger, grated
2 garlic cloves, crushed
2.5ml/¹⁄₂ tsp finely ground
  Sichuan peppercorns
15ml/1 tbsp light soy sauce
2.5ml/¹⁄₂ tsp caster (superfine) sugar
15ml/1 tbsp oyster sauce

Per portion Energy 102kcal/420kJ; Protein 3g; Carbohydrate 5g, of which sugars 4g; Fat 8g, of which saturates 2g; Cholesterol 0mg; Calcium 32mg; Fibre 1.1g; Sodium 425mg

Shredded aubergine

This dish of fried aubergine strips is traditionally served alongside fish. It is one of the most mouthwatering of western regional dishes, and is believed to have been a favourite of Empress Dowager Cixi whenever she travelled west to Zhongqing. She was frightened of being poisoned, so she would bring her own aubergines from the palace gardens. The reason for this paranoia was that she was not averse to poisoning anyone who crossed her!

1 Cut the aubergines or brinjals into strips about 6 x 2cm/2½ x ¾in. Heat the vegetable oil in a wok over a medium heat or in a deep-fryer and fry the aubergine strips, in batches if necessary, for 1–2 minutes, or until lightly browned. Lift out and drain on kitchen paper.

2 Heat the groundnut oil in a wok and fry the ginger, garlic and spring onions for 2 minutes. Add the soy sauce and wine or sherry and cook, stirring, for 1 minute.

3 Add the aubergine strips and chilli paste or sauce and stir-fry for 2 minutes. Put the cornflour in a small bowl and gradually blend with 30ml/2 tbsp water, then add to the wok.

4 Cook, stirring, until the sauce thickens to a glossy glaze that coats the aubergines. Serve immediately.

Serves 4

450g/1lb aubergines (eggplants)
  or Asian brinjals
vegetable oil, for deep-frying
30ml/2 tbsp groundnut (peanut) oil
25g/1oz fresh root ginger, finely grated
2 garlic cloves, crushed
2 spring onions (scallions), chopped
30ml/2 tbsp light soy sauce
30ml/2 tbsp Shaoxing wine or
  dry sherry
5ml/1 tsp hot chilli paste or sauce
5ml/1 tsp cornflour (cornstarch)
30ml/2 tbsp water

Cook's tip If you want the aubergines to absorb less oil, put the strips into a colander and sprinkle with salt. Leave for 30 minutes. Rinse, drain and dry the strips before deep-frying them. For an almost oil-free dish, plunge the aubergine strips into boiling water for 2 minutes, then drain thoroughly, instead of deep-frying them.

Per portion Energy 195kcal/805kJ; Protein 1g; Carbohydrate 5g, of which sugars 33g; Fat 18g, of which saturates 3g; Cholesterol 0mg; Calcium 21mg; Fibre 2.4g; Sodium 38mg

2 packets firm tofu (about 650g/
  1lb 7oz)
30ml/2 tbsp groundnut (peanut) oil
15ml/1 tbsp finely chopped garlic
1 fresh red chilli, finely chopped
5ml/1 tsp black bean sauce
30ml/2 tbsp sesame oil
30ml/2 tbsp chilli bean paste
  (dou banjiang)
200ml/7fl oz/scant 1 cup strong
  meat or vegetable stock
1 green (bell) pepper, finely diced
30ml/2 tbsp peas, thawed if frozen
5ml/1 tsp cornflour (cornstarch)
sliced spring onions (scallions),
  to garnish

Cook's tip You can use other
vegetables in this dish, if you like,
such as chopped spring onions,
leeks or carrots.

Pock-marked tofu

*Probably the best-known Sichuan export, this dish is now truly entrenched
in Chinese restaurants around the world, and it has fascinating etymology.
Legend has it that it was first cooked by a woman more than 100 years ago
in Chengdu. Her husband was a chef who was always experimenting with
new dishes, and when she cooked it for him he liked it so much that he
named it in her honour. A rather dubious compliment, but it has become
iconic nonetheless. There are many variations, some with minced pork or beef
and others with vegetarian ingredients, like this one, which uses peas.*

1 Cut the tofu into 2cm/³⁄₄in cubes. Spread out the cubes on a double layer of kitchen paper
to drain for 10 minutes – this makes them less prone to crumbling later.

2 Heat the oil in a wok over a medium-high heat. Add the garlic and chilli, and fry for
40 seconds. Add the black bean sauce, sesame oil and chilli bean paste. Stir for 1 minute,
then add the stock.

3 Bring to the boil, then add the tofu cubes, green pepper and peas. Cook for 2 minutes,
stirring gently, so that the tofu doesn't break up.

4 Put the cornflour in a small bowl and blend with 15ml/1 tbsp water. Add to the wok, then
stir until the sauce has thickened slightly. Serve immediately, garnished with spring onion slices.

Per portion Energy 276kcal/1143kJ; Protein 14g;
Carbohydrate 6g, of which sugars 3g; Fat 22g,
of which saturates 3g; Cholesterol 0mg;
Calcium 837mg; Fibre 1g; Sodium 365mg

Sweet things

In China, sweet dishes are rarely served as after-meal desserts. The tradition since ancient times has been for them to be served as sweet nibbles or snacks. Street hawkers in Chengdu and other provincial capitals can be seen selling a range of sugary dumplings and small bites, and, at grand banquets, a sweet dumpling may be served midway through the meal as a sort of palate cleanser. Few Chinese restaurants outside China offer these typical Chinese desserts, as many are acquired tastes.

Sugary treats and delicate creations

The products that go into sweet dishes include red or kidney beans, silver ear fungus (called bai mu erh in Mandarin), sesame seeds, tangerine peel, rock sugar and very little else. Tangerine peel is used widely in Hunan cooking, not just for sweet dishes but also with savoury meats and poultry dishes. Its citrus flavour is known for cutting the fat. Even Chinese herbalists sell it as an important medicinal herb for treating various illnesses.

Sesame seeds have a versatility all their own, and they are often ground for making the well-known dessert drink, Sesame Cream, which is enjoyed as a late-night snack. Both the white and black varieties are used in similar ways. They turn up often as a coating ingredient for battered and deep-fried foods.

Red beans are cooked and mashed with sugar as a filling for the famous pancakes that originated in Shanghai, though they are popular in western China, too. Used much like almond paste, it has a similar taste and texture to sweet chestnut purée and the Middle Eastern tahini.

Unlike many European desserts where wheat flour is the basic ingredient, rice flour plays the main role in this region. Rice flour balls are a favourite offering, believed to be of peasant origin, and are a featured dish in Hunan during festive days. Known as tong yuan, they are often tinted a delicate pink, as the colour symbolizes prosperity. The sugar syrup is also tinged with the citrus flavour of tangerine peel, which is very much a Hunan speciality.

Serves 4

350g/12oz/3 cups sesame seeds
115g/4oz/generous ½ cup caster
  (superfine) sugar
120ml/4fl oz/½ cup evaporated milk
15ml/1 tbsp cornflour (cornstarch)

Cook's tips
• If you prefer the cream less sweet, use ordinary milk instead of evaporated milk, but add it at the end of cooking and heat through, as it will curdle if overheated.
• Not all electric appliances can process such small ingredients as sesame seeds finely enough for this recipe. Grinding them first using a mortar and pestle helps.

Sesame cream

This is a universal Chinese dessert, which is actually more like a thick drink, and is sold by itinerant hawkers as a late-night snack. Many a mahjong player has been sustained through an all-night session with this sweet, warming cream. You find it in every province, especially Sichuan, where it is sometimes made with black sesame seeds. It is a very sweet dessert, so you may want to adjust the amount of sugar to your taste.

1 Put the sesame seeds into a food processor or blender with 350ml/12fl oz/1½ cups water and process until you get a smooth cream.

2 Put the sesame mixture in a pan with 600ml/1 pint/2½ cups water and bring to the boil. Simmer for 10 minutes over a low heat.

3 Add the sugar and evaporated milk, and stir until the sugar dissolves. Put the cornflour in a small bowl and gradually blend with 30ml/2 tbsp water, then add to the sesame mixture and cook until creamy and smooth.

Variation You can also use nuts for this recipe as they will grind down to the same consistency. Cashew nuts and almonds both work well and have very distinctive flavours.

Per portion Energy 695kcal/2890kJ; Protein 18g; Carbohydrate 37g, of which sugars 33g; Fat 54g, of which saturates 9g; Cholesterol 10mg; Calcium 677mg; Fibre 6.9g; Sodium 75mg

Red bean broth with tangerine

Tangerine peel is used widely in Hunan, not just for sweet dishes but also in meat and poultry recipes. Here it adds flavour to a broth of aduki beans and ginkgo nuts. Ginkgo nuts are known for their restorative properties and are often added to sweet brews.

1 Drain and rinse the beans, then put them in a medium pan and add 1 litre/1¾ pints/ 4 cups water. Bring to the boil and simmer for 15 minutes.

2 Add the tangerine peel and simmer for 10 minutes more, or until the beans are soft. Use a wooden spoon to mash them until they become a grainy paste.

3 Add the ginkgo nuts and their liquor, and the sugar, then cook for 5 minutes to make a broth. Taste and add more sugar if necessary.

Variation If you like, use canned lotus seeds or chopped Chinese dates instead of the ginkgo nuts.

Serves 4

150g/5oz dried aduki beans, soaked
  overnight until soft
1 small piece tangerine peel,
  5cm/2in square
115g/4oz canned ginkgo nuts
about 175g/6oz/scant 1 cup caster
  (superfine) sugar

Cook's tips

• If you have a pressure cooker, you can soak the beans in boiling water for 1 hour and then cook in the pressure cooker for 20 minutes.
• This broth is the basis of a sweet drink that is often served as a digestive after a surfeit of meat.

Per portion Energy 323kcal/1376kJ; Protein 8g; Carbohydrate 75g, of which sugars 49g; Fat 1g, of which saturates 0g; Cholesterol 0mg; Calcium 49mg; Fibre 5.3g; Sodium 7mg

Red bean paste pancakes

Pastes made with red beans and almonds are commonly used in Chinese sweet snacks and festive buns. Red bean paste is a typically Sichuan filling, used in many different ways, but this pancake is by far the most popular. They are eaten throughout China: in Shanghai these are called Shanghai pancakes and in Hong Kong they are called wo bing or wok pancakes. The custard powder gives the batter a good colour when fried.

1 Put the flour in a bowl and add the custard powder and beaten egg, then pour in 400ml/14fl oz/1²/₃ cups water and mix to form a batter with the consistency of thin cream. Strain into another bowl to remove any lumps.

2 Oil a sheet of baking parchment and a non-stick frying pan. Heat the pan and pour in 45ml/3 tbsp batter, swirling around the pan so that you get a round, thin pancake.

3 Cook until the underside is speckled with brown, then lift out and put on the baking parchment. Cover with a dish towel. Use the rest of the batter to make more pancakes.

4 When all the pancakes are cooked, spread a thin layer of bean paste in the centre of each (brown side up). Fold one side in to cover the filling and then fold in the other to overlap. Then tuck both ends under to seal and make a thin parcel.

5 Heat about 60ml/4 tbsp oil in the pan for shallow frying and cook each pancake, turning over once, until brown and crisp. Cool slightly and cut into slices to serve.

Variations
- Almond and chestnut purées also make excellent fillings, each with a different taste.
- Sprinkle fried pancakes, when still hot, with sesame seeds for extra crunch.

Makes 6 pancakes

150g/5oz/1¼ cups plain
  (all-purpose) flour
2.5ml/½ tsp custard powder
1 egg, lightly beaten
vegetable oil, for greasing and
  shallow frying
115g/4oz red bean paste

Cook's tip Red bean paste is easily available in Chinese stores.

Per portion Energy 186kcal/784kJ; Protein 5g; Carbohydrate 29g, of which sugars 7g; Fat 6g, of which saturates 1g; Cholesterol 39mg; Calcium 47mg; Fibre 1.5g; Sodium 17mg

Silver-ear fungus in rock sugar

Westerners who frequent Chinese restaurants often wonder why, despite the magnificent cuisine, there are so few desserts on offer. This has much to do with tradition: it is not within the culinary culture to serve sweet things after a meal. Most sweets are made only for festive occasions or as snacks. Also, many Chinese sweets use esoteric ingredients that are not well known in the West, such as the white or silver-ear fungus called bai mu erh in Mandarin, used in this recipe. Also called tremella mushrooms, they have a gelatinous texture and are delightfully crunchy.

1 Trim and discard the hard parts of the fungus, then cut into small pieces, wash and drain. Soak in warm water for about 20 minutes, until soft.

2 Put the fungus and sugar in a pan with 800ml/1¼ pints/3¼ cups water. Bring to the boil and simmer for 40 minutes, or until the fungus is jelly-like in texture.

3 Serve cold or warm.

Variation You could also add a few stoned (pitted) Chinese dates or slices of preserved and sweetened winter melon.

Serves 4

50g/2oz dried white fungus or
  silver-ear fungus
150g/5oz/3 cups rock sugar

Per portion Energy 109kcal/464kJ; Protein 1g; Carbohydrate 29g, of which sugars 20g; Fat 0g, of which saturates 0g; Cholesterol 0mg; Calcium 22mg; Fibre 0g; Sodium 5mg

Makes about 20 balls

200g/7oz/1¾ cups rice flour,
  plus extra for dusting
15g/½oz/2 tbsp tapioca flour
2.5ml/½ tsp salt
175ml/6fl oz/¾ cup tepid water
pinch of red colouring
150g/5oz/3 cups rock sugar
5cm/2in square piece of
  tangerine peel

Cook's tip With a few exceptions, most Chinese desserts are served hot. This one can be served hot or cold.

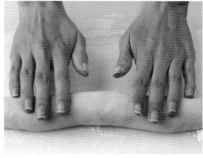

Per portion Energy 54kcal/228kJ; Protein 13g; Carbohydrate 4g, of which sugars 0g; Fat 0g, of which saturates 0g; Cholesterol 0mg; Calcium 3mg; Fibre 0.2g; Sodium 50mg

Rice-flour balls in sugar syrup

These tiny rice balls in a fragrant broth are known as tong yuan. Hunan cooks give the balls a delicate pink tint on special occasions, as the colour symbolizes prosperity. The sugar syrup is flavoured with tangerine peel.

1 Sift the two flours and the salt into a bowl and add the tepid water to make soft dough. Dissolve the red colouring in a little water and mix into the dough.

2 Divide the dough into two pieces and roll each on a floured board into a sausage shape about 2cm/1 in thick.

3 Pinch off small pieces the size of large grapes and shape them into round balls with your fingers.

4 Put 800ml/1¼ pints/3¼ cups water in a large pan and bring to the boil. Add the rock sugar and tangerine peel.

5 Drop in the balls and cook for 15 minutes. They will float to the surface when cooked. Serve hot.

Pearl balls

Although pearls are symbolic of longevity and beauty, this Sichuan dessert earned its name from the glistening sheen of the glutinous rice grains that coat these little dumplings. Short-grain glutinous rice grows best in mountainous areas, of which there are many in Sichuan province. These balls are filled with chestnut purée, making it a tasty fusion dish, which goes particularly well with ice cream.

1 Soak the rice for several hours or overnight in plenty of water. Sift the glutinous rice flour and rice flour together into a bowl and add the warm water. Stir to make a soft, pliable dough.

2 Divide the dough into two or three pieces and roll out on a floured board into sausage shapes about 2.5cm/1in wide. Cut off pieces the size of cherry tomatoes.

3 Flatten each piece and make a dent in the centre. Place 5ml/1 tsp chestnut purée in the centre and seal into balls. Roll to shape evenly like marbles.

4 Drain the glutinous rice grains thoroughly and put on a flat plate. Roll each dough ball around the rice to coat.

5 Arrange on a slightly oiled plate that is large enough to hold them without touching each other; they will swell slightly when steamed.

6 Put the plate in a wok or steamer over simmering water. Steam for 25 minutes, then serve warm.

Serves 4

90g/3½oz/½ cup short grain or
  ordinary glutinous rice
225g/8oz/2 cups glutinous rice flour,
  plus extra for dusting
15ml/1 tbsp rice flour
200ml/7fl oz/scant 1 cup
  warm water
115g/4oz/⅓ cup chestnut purée
cornflour (cornstarch), for coating

Cook's tip You can make the balls festive by tinting the glutinous rice red, blue or green with a little food colouring, if you like.

Per portion Energy 354kcal/1482kJ; Protein 6g;
Carbohydrate 76g, of which sugars 2g; Fat 2g,
of which saturates 2g; Cholesterol 0mg;
Calcium 32mg; Fibre 2.4g; Sodium 7mg

Suppliers

UNITED STATES

The House of Rice Store
3221 North Hayden Road
Scottsdale, AZ 85251
Tel: (480) 947 6698

99 Ranch Market
140 West Valley Boulevard
San Gabriel CA 91776
Tel: (626) 307 8899

Hong Kong Supermarket
18414 Colima Road,
Los Angeles CA 91748
Tel: (626) 964 1688

Seafood City Supermarket
1340, 3rd Avenue, Chula Vista
San Jose, CA 91911
Tel: (619) 422 7600

Ai Hoa
860 North Hill Street
Los Angeles, CA 90026
Tel: (213) 482 4824

Oriental Grocery
11827 Del Amo Boulevard
Cerritos, CA 90701
Tel: (310) 924 1029

Unimart American and
 Asian Groceries
1201 Howard Street
San Francisco, CA 94103
Tel: (415) 431 0326

Georgia Asian Foods, Etc.
1375 Prince Avenue
Atlanta, GA 30341
Tel: (404) 543 8624

Augusta Market Oriental Foods
2117 Martin Luther King
 Jr. Boulevard
Atlanta, GA 30901
Tel: (706) 722 4988

Hong Tan Oriental Food
2802 Capitol Street,
Savannah, GA 31404
Tel: (404) 233 6698

Khanh Tan Oriental Market
4051 Buford Highway NE
Atlanta, GA 30345
Tel: (404) 728 0393

Norcross Oriental Market
6062 Norcross-Tucker Road
Chamblee, GA 30341
Tel: (770) 496 1656

The Oriental Pantry
423 Great Road
Acton, MA 01720
Tel: (978) 264 4576

May's American Oriental
 Market
422 West University Avenue
Saint Paul, MN 55103
Tel: (651) 293 1118

Nevada Asian Market
2513 Stewart Avenue
Las Vegas, NV 89101
Tel: (702) 387 3373

Dynasty Supermarket
68 Elizabeth Street
New York, NY 10013
Tel: (212) 966 4943

Asian Supermarket
109 E. Broadway
New York, NY 10002
Tel: (212) 227 3388

Kam Man Food
 Products
200 Canal Street
New York, NY 10013
Tel: (212) 571 0330

Hang Hing Lee Grocery
33 Catherine Street
New York, NY 10013
Tel: (212) 732 0387

Oriental Market
670 Central Park Avenue
Yonkers, NY 10013
Tel: (212) 349 1979

Asian Foods Ltd
260–280 West Leigh Avenue
Philadelphia, PA 19133
Tel: (215) 291 9500

Golden Foods
 Supermarket
9896 Bellaire Road
Houston, TX 77036
Tel: (713) 772 7882

Welcome Food Centre
9810 Bellaire Boulevard
Houston, TX 77030
Tel: (718) 270 7789

UNITED KINGDOM

Wing Yip
375 Nechells Park Road, Nechells
Birmingham, B7 5NT
Tel: 0121 327 3838

Sing Fat Chinese Supermarket
334 Bradford Street, Digbeth
Birmingham, B5 6ES
Tel: 0121 622 5888

Makkah Oriental Food Store
148-150 Charminster Road
Bournemouth, BH8 8YY
Tel: 0120 277 7303

Ryelight Chinese Supermarket
48 Preston Street
Brighton, BN1 2HP
Tel: 0127 373 4954

Wai Yee Hong
Eastgate Oriental City
Eastgate Road, Eastville
Bristol, BS5 6XY
Tel: 0845 873 3388

Wing Yip
544 Purley Way,
Croydon, CR0 4NZ
Tel: 0208 688 4880

Hoo Hing Cash & Carry
Lockfield Avenue, Brimsdown
Enfield, EN3 7QE

Pat's Chung Ying Chinese
 Supermarket
199-201 Leith Walk
Edinburgh, EH6 8NX
Tel: 0131 554 0358

See Woo
Unit 5, The Point, 29, Saracen Street
Glasgow, G22 5H7
Tel: 0845 0788 818

Chung Ying Supermarket
254, Dobbies Loan
Glasgow, G4 OHS
Tel: 0141 333 0333

Rum Wong Supermarket
London Road
Guildford, GU1 2AF
Tel: 0148 345 1568

Seasoned Pioneers Ltd
101 Summers Road
Brunswick Business Park
Liverpool, L3 4BJ
Tel: 0151 709 9330

Loon Fung Supermarket
42–44 Gerrard Street
London, W1V 7LP
Tel: 0207 373 8305

New Loon Moon
 Supermarket
9a Gerrard Street
London, W1D 5PP
Tel: 0207 734 3887

Golden Gate Grocers
100–102 Shaftesbury Avenue
London, W1D 5EE
Tel: 0207 437 0014

New China Gate
18 Newport Place
London, WC1H 7PR
Tel: 0207 237 8969

New Peking Supermarket
59 Westbourne Grove
London, W2 4UA
Tel: 0207 928 8770

Newport Supermarket
28–29 Newport Court
London, WC2H 7PO
Tel: 0207 437 2386

See Woo Hong
18–20 Lisle Street
London, WC2H 7BA
Tel: 0207 439 8325

Wing Yip
395 Edgware Road
London, NW2 6LN
Tel: 0207 450 0422

Wing Yip
Oldham Road, Ancoats
Manchester, M4 5HU
Tel: 0161 832 3215

Woo Sang Supermarket
19–21 George Street, Chinatown
Manchester, M1 4HE
Tel: 0161 236 4353

Miah, A. and Co
20 Magdalen Street
Norwich, NR3 1HE
Tel: 0160 361 5395

Hoo Hing Commercial Centre
Freshwater Road
Chadwell Heath
Romford, RM8 1RX
Tel: 020 8548 3636
Website: www.hoohing.com

Wah-Yu Chinese Supermarket
145 High St
Swansea, SA1 1NE
Tel: 0179 265 0888

Hong Cheong
115 Oxford St
Swansea, SA1 3JJ
Tel: 0179 246 8411

Fox's Spices (mail order)
Mason's Road
Stratford-upon-Avon, CV37 9NF
Tel: 0178 926 6420

AUSTRALIA
Duc Hung Long Asian Store
95 The Crescent
Fairfield, NSW 2165
Tel: (02) 9728 1092

Foodtown Thai Kee Supermarket
393–399 Sussex Street
Sydney, NSW
Tel: (02) 9281 2202

Harris Farm Markets
Sydney Markets
Flemongton, NSW 2140
Tel: (02) 9746 2055

Asian Supermarkets Pty Ltd
116 Charters Towers Road
Townsville, QLD 4810
Tel: (07) 4772 3997

Burlington Supermarkets
Chinatown Mall
Fortitude Valley, QLD 4006
Tel: (07) 3216 1828

The Spice and Herb Asian Shop
200 Old Cleveland Road
Capalaba, QLD 4157
Tel: (07) 3245 5300

Western Australia Kongs
 Trading Pty Ltd
8 Kingscote Street
Kewdale, WA 6105
Tel: (08) 9353 3380

NEW ZEALAND
Golden Gate Supermarket &
 Wholesalers Ltd.
8–12 Teed Street, Newmarket
Auckland Tel: (09) 523 3373

Happy Super Market
660 Dominion Road,
Mt Roskill,
Auckland Tel: (09) 623 8220

Lim Garden Supermarket Centre
3 Edsel Street, Henderson,
Auckland Tel: (09) 835 2599

CANADA
Arirang Oriental Food Store
1324 10 Ave Sw # 30
Calgary, AB, T3C 0J2
Tel: (403) 228 0980

T & T Supermarket
222 Cherry Street
Toronto, ON, M5A 3L2
Tel: (416) 463 8113
Website: www.tnt-supermarket.com
(16 stores across the country)

Marché Hawai
1999 Marcel Laurin, Sain-Laurent
Montreal, QC
Tel: (514) 856 0226

Hing Shing Market
1757 Kingsway, Vancouver, BC
Tel: (604) 873 4938

Star Asian Food Centre
2053 41st Avenue
W Vancouver, BC
Tel: (604) 263 2892

Tin Cheung Market
6414 Victoria Drive
Vancouver, BC
Tel: (604) 322 9237

Western Oriental Market
101–1050 Kingsway
Vancouver, BC
Tel: (604) 876 4711

Wing Sang Meat & Vegetable Market
3755 Main Street
Vancouver, BC
Tel: (604) 879 6866

Index

Publisher's acknowledgements
The publisher would also like to
thank the following for permission
to reproduce their images (t = top,
b = bottom, l = left, r = right): p6l
TAO Images Limited/Alamy; p6r
Antony Ratcliffe/Alamy; p8l
iStockphoto; p8r Carl & Ann Purcell/
Corbis; p9t Victor Paul Borg/Alamy;
p9b Zhai Dong Feng/Redlink/Corbis;
p10l Imagemore Co. Ltd./Alamy;
p10r and p11l Eye Ubiquitous/
Alamy; p11r and p12r Robert
Harding Picture Library Ltd/Alamy;
p12l Yiap Kappa Files/Alamy; p13t
China Daily/Reuters/Corbis; p13b
Stringer Shanghai/Reuters/Corbis.